I0759563

SMALL GARDEN ENVY

SMALL GARDEN ENVY

FOLKO KULLMANN
With photographs by Marianne Majerus

Contents

Small is Beautiful

Creating an alluring outdoor retreat, however small, is easier than you think.

Who doesn't want an enviable garden? For most of us these days, if we are lucky enough to have a garden at all, space is often at a premium. But with smart design choices, even a small garden can feel spacious, stylish and functional, and you don't need to have a huge bank account to achieve it.

Browsing magazines or online for inspiration, you will quickly be overwhelmed by a dizzying array of stunning gardens, skilfully designed, expertly planted and beautifully decorated. But which is the best one for you? We have curated 47 small gardens to suit all tastes, embracing a wide range of styles and that are adaptable for different situations.

Whether you would like a natural garden for wildlife, favour a more formal design approach, are looking to create a stylish space to relax and entertain or want ideas for greening a balcony or roof terrace, we have the right plan for you. Created by some of the best garden designers in the business, our featured gardens offer plenty of inspiration and we'll show you how to affordably recreate the look.

The gardens are grouped by theme so you can easily identify what will work best for your space: outdoor living; balconies and roof terraces; informal and natural gardens; structured gardens and practical gardens with fun ideas for children. To help you plant the right garden for your geographical location, you will find a list of suitable plants and requirements at the back of the book.

Designing Small Gardens

With careful planning, even the tiniest plot can be transformed. The key to a successful design is to balance structure, scale and layers to create depth and interest.

1. Define the space

Structure is essential in small gardens. Without it, they can feel cluttered rather than inviting. Use hedges, trellises or pergolas to divide the space into different zones, creating a sense of depth and enclosure. Vertical elements, such as climbing plants or tall, narrow trees like Italian cypress (*Cupressus sempervirens*), can add height without taking up valuable ground space. Arches or arbours positioned at key points create a sense of adventure and discovery, leading the eye through the garden.

2. Keep it cohesive

A unified design makes a small garden feel more spacious. Limiting the colour palette to a few complementary shades prevents visual overload, while repeating materials such as stone, wood or gravel in hardscaping maintains a sense of harmony. The same principle applies to planting: grouping plants with similar textures and forms can help create a cohesive, tranquil atmosphere. Keeping furniture, pots and decorative elements in a similar style ensures a seamless blend between garden features.

3. Boundaries and perspective

One way to create the illusion of more space is to use different heights of plants. Place taller ones at the back and lower ones at the front to create depth and layers. You can also use grasses like hakone grass (*Hakonechloa macra*) and plants such as lavender and thyme to soften the edges of borders and paths for a more integrated look.

A few simple design tricks can make a small garden look much larger. Throw in some diagonal pathways to lead the eye and create a sense of movement; use features beyond your garden, like buildings or tall trees, to produce a 'borrowed landscape'; and add a focal point such as a seat, sculpture, water feature or solitary tree. Mirrors or reflective surfaces along walls can be deadly for birds who fly into them, so it's best to avoid using them.

4. Choose your plants wisely

Every plant in a small garden should have a purpose. Choose those that will provide interest throughout the year: evergreens give structure, perennials add colour and climbers can be used on walls without taking up space on the ground. Choose trees or shrubs with multiple interesting features like flowers, foliage, bark, growth and autumn colours – such as maples (*Acer*), dogwood (*Cornus*) or magnolias. Fine-textured plants, like airy ornamental grasses or bamboos, make the space feel open without being overcrowded. When you're picking plants, always check how they grow: it's better to have compact, slow-growing varieties rather than those that spread a lot and take over the space.

This especially applies to bamboos: always choose clump-forming species like *Fargesia* rather than the spreading *Phyllostachys* species unless you keep it contained in a pot.

The legendary English garden designer Beth Chatto devised the principle of 'right plant, right place': following this advice ensures that plants thrive naturally in your garden, reducing maintenance and use of resources. Getting plants to look their best is most easily achieved by choosing those that are right for your garden situation and local climate conditions.

5. Embrace multifunctionality

In small spaces, every element needs to work harder. Built-in seating with hidden storage, foldable tables or fire pits that also double as coffee tables are great for making the most of the space. Raised beds can be used as retaining walls or for extra seating. Water features add movement and sound while taking up hardly any room. Smart, adaptable design makes the most of every square metre.

These garden 'rooms' blur the boundary between inside and outside, providing the perfect space for entertaining and relaxing.

OUTDOOR LIVING

1.

Cool exotic
Combine modern materials and natural planting to create a chic outdoor retreat.

This stylish garden exemplifies a clean and structured design, combining contemporary materials with thoughtful planting. The smooth concrete paving provides a sleek and durable surface and the cool tones are repeated in the raised beds and furniture, creating a cohesive and understated colour scheme.

The palm tree introduces a bold, architectural element, bringing a tropical atmosphere and adding texture to the space. Its glossy, feathered fronds contrast with the matte, linear forms of the hard landscaping, giving a more exotic feel.

A striking metal wall panel with intricate cut-out silhouettes serves as a focal point. This adds visual interest and provides a subtle screen for privacy, blending functionality with design. Dark grey woven chairs with matching cushions and a simple black side table offer a comfortable and sophisticated seating area. The arrangement is complemented by a plush, textured pouffe, introducing a subtle pop of colour without disrupting the garden's overall harmony.

Cranesbill like *Geranium* 'Rozanne' softens the planting beds with its vibrant blue blooms, adding seasonal interest and enhancing the planting design. Its trailing habit provides a pleasing contrast with the more structural forms of the raised bed.

Achieve a cool exotic look

Above Chinese windmill palm (*Trachycarpus fortunei*).

Include palms

Palms are the go-to plants for introducing a tropical vibe. Hardy species like Chinese windmill palms (*Trachycarpus fortunei* and *wagnerianus*) are evergreens that bring height and visual interest with their bold, fan-shaped leaves. Ideal for compact gardens, these exotic plants can thrive even in cooler climates.

Cool colour palette

A palette of cool tones evokes a sense of calm while enhancing the modern aesthetic. Use grey concrete for paths and patios, blue-green foliage plants like blue fescue (*Festuca glauca*) and turquoise accents in cushions or planters to tie the look together.

Natural materials

Incorporating natural materials adds texture and warmth to the structured design, ensuring the space feels grounded and inviting. Add stone and gravel for paths and borders, wood for benches, decking or trellises and sculptural elements like driftwood or weathered logs as focal points.

Open spaces

Maintain a sense of openness by choosing light, minimalist furniture, using airy plants like grasses or gaura (*Oenothera lindheimeri*) for movement without heaviness and keeping borders and pathways uncluttered.

Seasonal interest

While this garden's core aesthetic is evergreen and consistent, adding seasonal accents keeps the space engaging year-round. These can be flowering plants: incorporate long-blooming perennials like cranesbill (*Geranium* 'Rozanne'), or seasonal exotics like canna lilies for bursts of colour. Grasses provide autumn highlights: the foliage of Chinese silver grass (*Miscanthus sinensis*) or switch grass (*Panicum virgatum*) takes on warm, golden hues in the autumn.

Accessories are also an easy way to change the look of your garden: rotate textiles like cushions and blankets in seasonal shades for a refreshing update.

GARDEN FEATURES

Ⓐ Lightweight, easy-to-move furniture allows maximum flexibility.

Ⓑ The seating is made from weatherproof recycled fibres for longevity outdoors.

Ⓒ Grey cushions fit in with the colour scheme and provide comfort while being weatherproof.

Ⓓ Palm trees like this Chinese windmill palm (*Trachycarpus fortunei*) prefer temperate climates and part shade.

Ⓔ The zinc-finished metal wall with its cut-out silhouettes allows glimpses of the landscape beyond while creating privacy.

Ⓕ Perennials like the ever-blooming cranesbill (*Geranium* 'Rozanne') create almost year-round interest.

Ⓖ A textured pouffe provides extra comfort and a pop of complementary colour.

Ⓗ Low-maintenance concrete pavers give a cool and modern effect.

2.

Herbal patio

Balance fragrant planting and structured design for a functional entertaining space.

This narrow garden is a perfect blend of structural and natural elements. The brick paving, arranged in a neat pattern, provides a solid foundation that guides movement through the space. Its neutral tones blend well with the surrounding greenery and planting.

Under the canopy of a magnolia tree, *Hydrangea arborescens* 'Annabelle' grows, producing clusters of white flowers. The round flower heads complement the elegant blossoms of the magnolias.

The timber seating arrangement with neutral cushions offers a comfortable space for relaxation, the wood tones integrating smoothly with the garden's overall design, while the gridded windows of the conservatory provide a sleek, minimalist backdrop. Terracotta pots with tomato plants introduce a practical feature within the design.

Lavender and other herbs along the borders add texture and provide a subtle fragrance, delightful when lounging outdoors on summer evenings. Their purple flowers and silvery foliage soften the garden's edges, and as they grow fairly compactly they are unlikely to overwhelm the space. Planting herbs such as lavender, rosemary and mint can help to repel garden mosquitoes, while others, like basil, thyme and oregano, will attract beneficial pollinators.

Designs for long, narrow gardens

Break up the space

Long gardens can feel like corridors if left unstructured. Introducing divisions such as low hedging, trellis panels or planting pockets helps to break the linear view and create a sense of progression. Subtle transitions between 'rooms' or zones give each section its own atmosphere, from dining area to shady retreat or flower border.

Use diagonal lines and curves

Rather than emphasizing the garden's length with straight paths and beds, use diagonal stepping stones, offset planting or curved or rectangular borders to redirect the eye. These visually widen the space and soften the layout, making the garden feel broader.

Vary height and texture

Layered planting is especially important in narrow gardens. Use a mix of canopy trees, mid-level shrubs, perennials and ground covers to create depth along both sides. Vertical interest – whether through climbing plants, tall grasses or raised containers – helps draw attention upwards.

Create focal points

Add a focal feature at the far end – such as a bench, sculpture or striking plant – with smaller secondary focal points, like large pots or water features, placed along the way to guide the view and create a sense of journey. The key is to lead the eye through the garden without revealing everything at once.

Play with light and contrast

Long gardens often have uneven light, with sun at one end or side and shade at the other. Use planting to respond to these shifts: sun-loving species like lavender and rosemary can thrive in the brightest areas, while shade-tolerant plants such as Japanese anemone (*Anemone hupehensis*) or ferns create cool, restful zones. Contrasts in foliage colour and texture – silver against deep green, fine against bold – add richness and interest to the planting.

Right Japanese anemone (*Anemone hupehensis*).

GARDEN FEATURES

Ⓐ The soft, earthy tones of the brick paving create a warm, textural surface that unifies the planting and seating zones.

Ⓑ Lavender (*Lavandula angustifolia*) planted in rhythmic clusters along the path adds scent, structure and seasonal colour.

Ⓒ Hydrangea (*Hydrangea arborescens* 'Annabelle') produces large, luminous flower heads that lend a classic, romantic touch.

Ⓓ A magnolia flourishes in dappled shade and provides a leafy screen beside the seating area.

Ⓔ Himalayan birch (*Betula utilis* subsp. *jacquemontii*) thrives in full sun and features a striking bark and fluttering foliage.

Ⓕ Comfortable lounge seating area.

Ⓖ Potted herbs and tomatoes near the house bring planting close to the living space, with the flexibility to be refreshed throughout the seasons.

Ⓗ A water feature adds a gentle, calming sound that masks background noise and attracts birds.

Ⓘ Evergreen shrubs such as boxwood (*Buxus sempervirens*) and pittosporum (*Pittosporum tobira*) anchor the planting and provide year-round texture.

3.

Pink paradise
Blend interesting materials, strong colour and formal planting for a low-maintenance but lively garden.

This compact courtyard at the back of a souterrain (lower ground floor) apartment makes bold use of colour and materials to create a vibrant, inviting space. The bright pink walls are a striking backdrop, adding energy to the greenery and soft planting.

To the left, an integrated, multitiered container arrangement featuring bellflowers and clematis brings vertical interest. The pale purple tones of the bellflowers blend with the richer blue of the clematis, standing out against the vivid walls. A cube-shaped evergreen boxwood introduces a more formal element and gives privacy, screening the steps that lead to street level.

The use of wooden decking adds warmth and texture, complementing the bold colours and soft planting. Large sliding glass doors seamlessly connect the interior living space with the garden, creating a fluid transition between inside and out.

The zinc wall cover adds a contemporary, industrial feel. Its cool, metallic surface contrasts with the bright pink walls and soft planting, enhancing the garden's quirky, modern aesthetic.

Easy wins for souterrain gardens

Keep it minimal

By reducing decorative clutter and focusing on clean forms, such as geometric containers or clipped evergreens, the space feels more open and composed. Structured planting has room to shine without being overshadowed by ornamentation.

Balance bold colour with cool tones

Strong colours, like these vibrant pink walls, can bring energy to lower ground-level gardens. To keep things balanced, combine them with cooler tones: silvery green foliage, deep purples and blue flowering perennials, as well as the zinc walls, all help soften the scheme.

Moderate temperature

Sunken gardens naturally benefit from thermal mass: in other words, the surrounding walls and soil help buffer against temperature extremes. On hot days, they remain cooler than street-level spaces, offering shade and respite.

Use horizontal lines

Timber decking boards and long, raised beds reinforce the horizontal perspective to expand the view. This visual stretching effect helps counter the vertical compression often felt in sunken gardens, making the space feel broader. When using reclaimed timber you get the advantage of an aged look that tells its own story.

Plant for shade tolerance

These spaces often receive filtered or reflected light. Choose plants that thrive in partial shade such as ferns, sedges (*Carex*), lilyturf (*Liriope muscari*) and clematis. These species retain good structure, offer varied texture and remain attractive through the seasons.

Play with levels

Terracing or level changes such as steps or tiered planters help organize the space and create rhythm. Elevated elements, like boxwood cubes or trained trees, draw the eye upwards and help screen boundaries, creating depth and privacy.

Left *Clematis* 'The President'.

GARDEN FEATURES

Ⓐ Modern, zinc-finished metal raised beds define planting areas and contribute to the clean, structured design.

Ⓑ Warm wooden decking softens the bold colour scheme and provides a functional, level surface.

Ⓒ Vertical greenery, like clematis, softens the walls and adds depth to the space.

Ⓓ A cube-shaped evergreen boxwood (*Buxus sempervirens*) mirrors the garden's geometric forms, giving a unified feel.

Ⓔ The zinc wall is corrosion-resistant and doesn't need frequent upkeep. Its slightly reflective surface makes the small space feel bigger and brighter.

Ⓕ Evergreen, shade-loving plants such as sedges (*Carex*) or lilyturf (*Liriope muscari*) provide year-round greenery and thrive in low-light conditions.

Ⓖ Slim, trained trees like these pears along the back border offer privacy and soften boundary lines.

Ⓗ Floor-to-ceiling glass doors maximize natural light and create indoor–outdoor flow, ideal for entertaining.

Urban fireplace
Enjoy a warm welcome with a carefully composed garden that makes the most of a narrow plot.

At the heart of this garden, a simple metal fire bowl provides a central focal point, extending the garden's usability into cooler evenings. Portable fire bowls, like this one, work well for small gardens, allowing flexibility in layout. Choose materials like steel, cast iron, stone or concrete for both durability and aesthetic appeal.

Closest to the house, smooth stone slabs connect the indoor and outdoor spaces. These transition into a strip of concrete cobblestones, guiding movement into the garden, while further along, a gravel surface softens the space, lending an informal contrast to the structured layout. Comfortable woven loom sofas in earth tones, positioned on either side of the fire bowl, provide a relaxed seating arrangement.

Topiaried evergreen shrubs are strategically placed, adding formal structure and year-round interest. Wooden lattice borders offer privacy while supporting climbing plants, adding vertical interest without feeling closed in. Apple trees introduce height and seasonal colour, providing dappled shade and enhancing the layered design. They are symmetrically positioned to frame the different garden 'rooms'. Their long and slender trunks allow the eye to explore the areas beyond, thus creating the illusion of a much larger space.

GARDEN FEATURES

- (A) Smooth stone slabs create a solid transition between indoor and outdoor spaces.
- (B) Concrete cobblestones drain well, minimizing the risk of flooding after a downpour.
- (C) Gravel surfacing adds an informal contrast and is comfortable to walk on.
- (D) A metal fire bowl serves as a focal point. Always place fire bowls on a heat-resistant surface like gravel, stone or bricks. Light stone or wood is less suitable as it can be soiled by ashes. Keep a distance of at least 50cm (1½ft) between any plants and the heat source.
- (E) Comfortable woven sofas are positioned a metre (3–4ft) away from the fire for safety.
- (F) Round evergreen shrubs (yew and boxwood are ideal) introduce structure and year-round interest.
- (G) Wooden lattice borders enclose the garden and support climbing plants. Evergreen choices include ivy or honeysuckle, while clematis has beautiful flowers and seedheads, and grapevine brings colourful foliage and tasty fruits in autumn.
- (H) In small gardens, opt for multitasking tree species. These apple trees start the season with bright pinkish-white flowers, have lush green leaves during summer and provide fresh apples in autumn.

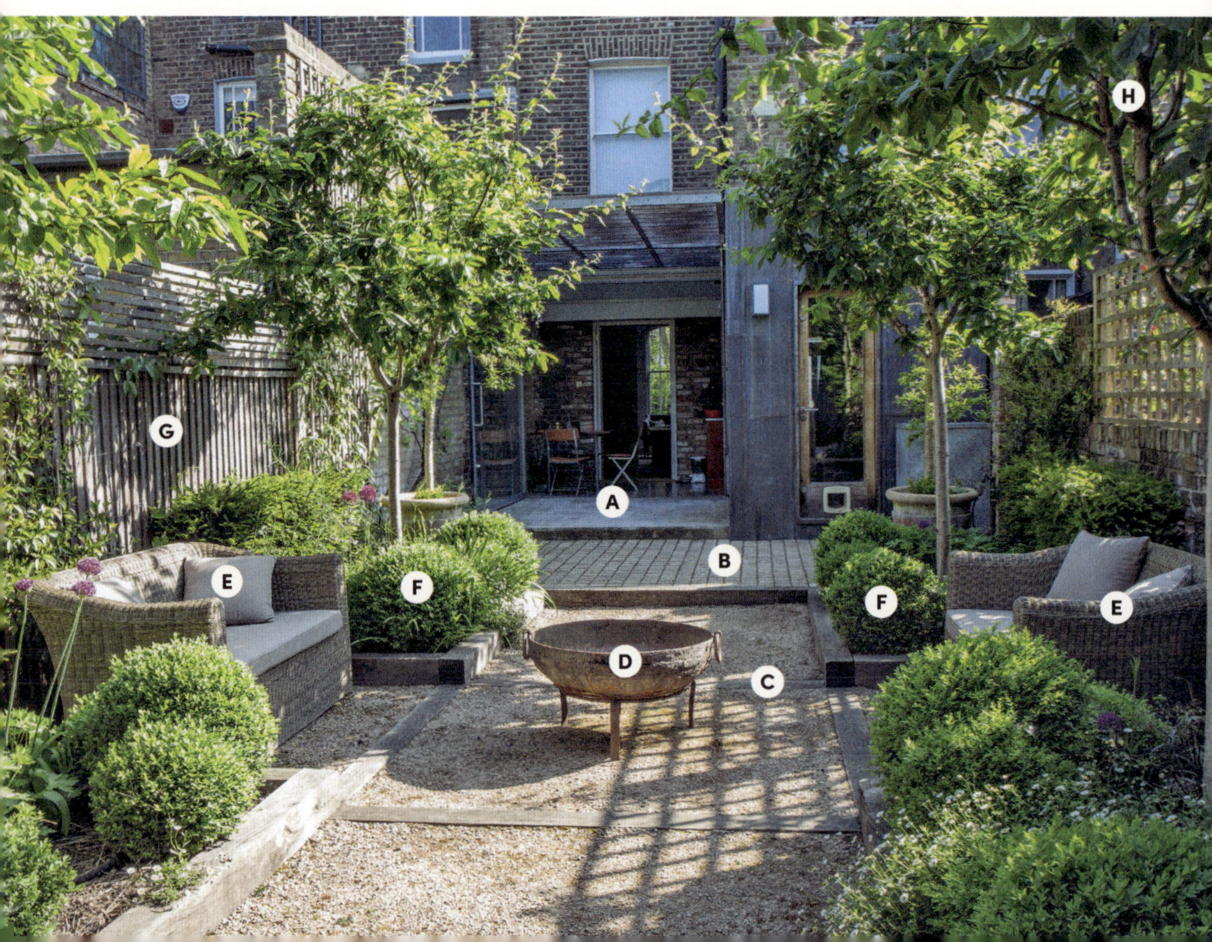

Above Honeysuckle (*Lonicera*).

Above Apple blossom (*Malus domestica*).

Best surface materials for decks and paths

MATERIAL	USE	SPECIAL FEATURES
Stone slabs	Terrace and seating, paths	Large slabs can create a grander atmosphere and make an area appear more spacious.
Cobblestone	Terrace and seating, paths	Great for DIY projects; enormous variety of stone types to choose from.
Finestone	Terrace and seating	Allows water to drain through its surface, reducing run-off and helping to prevent waterlogging.
Gravel	Seating, paths	Ideal for areas near the house as larger gravel is not so easily carried into the living area.
Sand	Paths	Easily maintained; will acquire a nice 'plant patina' over time.

5.

Sunken seating
Create a cosy and intimate space for meditative moments or social gatherings.

This garden features a sunken seating area surrounded by vibrant perennials and ornamental grasses. The design utilizes the ground depth instead of width, maximizing space, and the lowered level gives a sense of enclosure, making the area feel private and inviting. This multifunctional space is ideal for intimate gatherings, relaxation and meditation, and the sunken design provides a natural windbreak for a cosy feel.

The planting scheme bursts with colour, blending warm hues of orange, red and yellow with cooler blues and greens, offering visual interest throughout the seasons. The dark wooden fence provides a strong, grounding backdrop that enhances the brightness of the surrounding plants.

A sleek metal pergola frames the seating area, topped with a terracotta-coloured canopy that softens the light and offers shelter. This warm tone is echoed in the floral palette and the accent cushions on the lounge chairs, creating a harmonious design.

Lounge chairs with comfortable cushions and pillows invite relaxation, while a low table adds practicality. The thoughtful combination of textures and colours ensures this garden is both restful and visually stimulating.

GARDEN FEATURES

(A) Lounge chairs with removable cushions are an inviting space to relax.

(B) Stretched across the pergola, the canopy provides shade and ties in with the colour palette.

(C) The dark wooden fence provides enclosure and a contrasting backdrop to set off the bright planting.

(D) The low wall topped with stone slabs functions as additional seating.

(E) Pheasant's tail grass (*Anemanthele lessoniana*) offers soft, flowing texture with copper-toned leaves that complement the garden's colour scheme.

(F) Yellow-green spurges (*Euphorbias*) provide structure and a vibrant pop of colour.

(G) A small multistemmed birch tree (*Betula*) offers dappled shade, shelter and privacy while softening the garden's structure.

(H) The sunken level allows for full immersion in the surroundings. Thanks to its sheltered location, it warms up during the course of the day and so is ideal for relaxing in the evening. A sunken garden is perfect for cultivating tender plants that don't like cold or chilly winds.

Make the most of small seating areas

Privacy first
Tall planting and the dark wooden back fence provide privacy from the sides and above, creating a secluded atmosphere.

Surrounded by plants
Dense planting of flowers and grasses envelops the seating area, creating a lush, transparent look that softens the garden's structure. This makes the garden appear larger as you can glimpse through the plants, in contrast with solid walls or fences that shield the surroundings from view.

Cohesive colour scheme
Greys and warm orange-red tones, paired with touches of blue, unify this design. The scheme is carried through the flowers, the terracotta canopy of the pergola and the accent cushions.

Wildlife habitat
The diverse planting attracts pollinators like bees and butterflies, creating a calming soundscape filled with gentle humming and buzzing. Here, umbellifers like *Cortia wallichiana*; yellow, orange and red yarrows (*Achilleas*) and bright yellowish-green spurges (*Euphorbias*) attract wild bees, hover flies and butterflies.

Soften hard edges with plants
Overhanging branches and cascading foliage soften the rigid lines of the walls and seating area, blending the built environment with the natural planting.

Top Yarrow (*Achillea*). **Bottom** Spurge (*Euphorbia*).

6.

Tropical serenity
An interplay of bold foliage, soft grasses and clean architectural lines creates a calm and considered retreat.

This stylish courtyard garden blends lush greenery with structured design. Tree ferns introduce architectural height and texture, their broad fronds casting dappled shade. These bold plants contrast with the soft clumps of hakone grass, which add a feeling of movement and vibrancy.

Carefully clipped spherical topiary shrubs offer formal structure, balancing the garden's natural softness with defined shapes. The planting palette is intentionally restrained, focusing on green tones and texture to cultivate a sense of calm and cohesion.

An elevated seating area with built-in wooden benches serves as the garden's focal point, providing both structure and functionality. Cushions in subtle tones offer comfort while maintaining the garden's minimalist aesthetic.

Horizontal lattice borders echo the colour of the timber decking, integrating the vertical and horizontal elements. These borders add formality while supporting climbing plants, subtly enclosing the space without making it feel confined.

Create a lush look

Stick to green
A unified palette of greens gives a verdant feel, while natural materials like wood for flooring and garden borders enhance the jungle-like atmosphere.

Exotic plants
Tree ferns, palms and broad-leaved shrubs introduce bold, tropical textures that create visual impact. Chinese windmill palms (*Trachycarpus fortunei*) add vertical structure with their fan-shaped leaves, while the *Dicksonia antarctica* soft tree fern brings a lush, prehistoric feel with its dense, arching fronds. Shrubs like yulan (*Magnolia denudata*) contribute elegant, sculptural forms and seasonal interest with their striking leaves and white flowers. When using bamboo species like *Phyllostachys* that form runners from their rhizomes, ensure that these are kept in check by a rhizome barrier.

Bold forms
Combining soft, flowing grasses with structured, clipped shrubs adds dynamic contrast and balance. Some ideally suited shrubs include boxwood (*Buxus sempervirens*), yew (*Taxus*) and sweet olive (*Osmanthus*).

Create a canopy
Layered planting with exotic shrubs and fast-growing trees provides overhead greenery, fostering a sheltered, intimate feel. Trees like princess tree (*Paulownia*) and Indian bean tree (*Catalpa*) grow quickly and can be pruned to maintain a desired height. These species also respond well to coppicing – being cut back hard to the ground every one to three years – which encourages vigorous regrowth with impressively large leaves.

Above Soft tree fern (*Dicksonia antarctica*).

Seasonal interest
Minimalist accents like decorative objects or cushions subtly introduce colour and texture without overwhelming the space.

GARDEN FEATURES

(A) A natural timber deck creates a warm transition between indoors and the garden, enhancing the flow and functionality.

(B) Neatly pruned boxwood shrubs provide year-round structure and contrast with the softer planting, reinforcing the formal elements.

(C) Positioned as focal points, tree ferns introduce lush, exotic foliage that adds height and a sense of enclosure.

(D) Tall and slender bamboo provides vertical interest and a soft rustling sound, contributing to a serene atmosphere.

(E) A horizontal timber lattice mirrors the deck's material and offers support for climbing plants, blending structure with greenery.

(F) The integrated wooden bench, crafted from the same material as the decking, provides seating.

(G) Clumps of hakone grass (*Hakonechloa macra*) introduce movement and softness, contrasting with the structured elements.

7.

Minimal courtyard

Geometric forms and evergreen planting combine in a cool and contemporary space.

The multilevel layout of this elegant courtyard garden really makes the most of a compact space and creates clearly defined zones. The lower level provides an enclosed seating area for outdoor dining, while the upper terrace provides additional gathering space in a Zen-style garden. The formal dining table and benches harmonize with the clean architectural lines of the garden.

Smooth finestone stairs lead to the upper level, where a narrow strip of grass softens the transition between levels. Evergreen African lilies line both the lower and upper terraces, their architectural forms providing continuity and texture year-round.

Carefully clipped boxwood spheres introduce soft, sculptural shapes that contrast with the linear structure of the garden. This organic form is balanced by a precisely clipped rectangular yew hedge on the right, echoing the sharp lines of the stairs and seating area.

An evergreen climber drapes the rear wall without crowding the space. On the upper level, the airy canopy of an antarctic beech introduces height and delicate texture, casting light shade over the space below.

GARDEN FEATURES

Ⓐ Topiaried boxwood (*Buxus sempervirens*) shrubs provide soft, rounded shapes, offering a contrast to the many angular lines.

Ⓑ A lawn on the upper level softens the hardscape and provides a fresh green accent and contrast to the light beige stairs and walls.

Ⓒ A sharply defined yew (*Taxus baccata*) hedge mirrors the architectural lines, introducing formality and structure.

Ⓓ Evergreen African lily (*Agapanthus*) offers year-round texture and softens the different levels.

Ⓔ Evergreen climbing plants add vertical greenery, enhancing privacy and blending architecture with nature.

Ⓕ The delicate, airy habit of antarctic beech *(Nothofagus antarctica)* introduces height and texture, casting light shade over the garden.

Ⓖ Smooth concrete steps provide a clean transition between garden levels.

Ⓗ The simple and elegant seating, crafted from natural wood, complements the garden's refined design.

Create a minimalist aesthetic

Elegant materials

Fine-grained concrete, light wood and slim metal frames contribute to a sleek, modern look. Using materials with subtle textures adds visual interest without overloading the minimalist design. Concrete surfaces provide a clean foundation, while natural wood introduces warmth and softness.

Less is more

Be reductive in your choice of plants. A limited selection creates a focused, uncluttered design. Carefully chosen specimens emphasize form and structure, allowing each plant to stand out. This approach reduces maintenance and keeps the garden looking polished throughout the year.

Evergreens for year-round interest

Shrubs like yew, laurel (*Laurus nobilis*) and Christmas berry (*Photinia*) ensure structure and greenery throughout the year. Their foliage offers a consistent backdrop to seasonal changes like the appearance of the white and blue flowers of the African lily, providing stability and visual continuity across all seasons.

Above African lily (*Agapanthus*).

Sculptural forms

Clipped and pruned shrubs introduce formality and contrast with softer plantings. Geometric shapes like spheres and rectangles create a sense of order, highlighting the architectural hardscaping of the garden.

Refined colour palette

Restrained use of light, neutral colours maintains a calm atmosphere. Avoid using bold or bright tones. Soft greens, greys and natural wood tones create harmony, allowing the garden's forms and textures to take centre stage. Stark white should be avoided as it can be uncomfortable to look at on a bright summer's day.

8.

Inside out

Bold colours, structured forms and layered planting produce a dynamic indoor-outdoor retreat.

This contemporary courtyard garden is truly an extension of the indoor living space. Large-format stone slabs that match the interior flooring create a seamless transition between the two areas, separated by elegant glass doors.

A striking blue lounge sofa in the garden introduces bold colour, providing a vibrant contrast to the surrounding greenery. The colour scheme is echoed further by decorative elements within the house to tie the two spaces together.

Precisely clipped, spherical yew shrubs provide formal structure. A round beech introduces seasonal colour, turning a rich bronze in autumn. The vertical structure of the garden is defined by a Persian ironwood, which provides height, fiery young foliage in spring and later brilliant autumn foliage of red and gold. Known for its tolerance to heat and drought, this species is ideal for warmer urban gardens with limited access to water.

An evergreen honeysuckle climbs along the walls, providing privacy and shelter for birds, while softening the structural edges of the garden with its lush foliage.

Link inside and out

Align materials and finishes
Continuity of surface materials is an effective way to link interior and exterior spaces. Use similar or complementary flooring, such as timber decking that echoes indoor wooden floors or stone tiles with the same tone and texture inside and out.

Blur boundaries
Glazed sliding or folding doors open wide to dissolve the threshold between house and garden. When retracted, they connect the two spaces, transforming the garden into an extension of the living room. Even when closed, they maintain a strong connection with the landscape.

Extend the colour palette
Use echoes of the interior colour scheme in the garden through planters, furniture, cushions or painted walls. Likewise, indoor fabrics and textures can be mirrored in outdoor furniture or rugs to subtly bridge the divide.

Frame garden views
Design focal points within the garden that are visible from key spots inside the home. A sculptural tree, planted container, fireplace or water feature draws the eye, encouraging interaction between indoors and out.

Match functions across the threshold
Think about how spaces are used and pair interior and exterior zones with similar functions. A kitchen might open onto a herb garden or dining terrace, while a lounge area can lead to a sheltered patio. Mirroring these functions helps integrate daily routines across both spaces, enhancing usability.

Left Persian ironwood tree (*Parrotia persica*).

GARDEN FEATURES

(A) A modern fireplace is the central feature at the end of the garden, signalling that this is a functional living space.

(B) Smooth paving connects the indoor and outdoor areas, enhancing flow.

(C) The vibrant sofa adds a contemporary pop of colour. The use of the same shades inside and out links the two areas.

(D) A rounded beech (*Fagus sylvatica*) provides structure and seasonal colour.

(E) The yew (*Taxus baccata*) globe is low-maintenance, needing to be clipped only once a year. The fresh, light green shoots bring a splash of colour to the design scheme.

(F) Persian ironwood (*Parrotia persica*) adds vertical interest with brilliant autumn colour.

(G) Pear trees (*Pyrus communis*) trained to grow flat against the brick wall provide both fruit and visual interest without taking up much space. The wall retains heat, helping pears ripen and protecting them from frost.

(H) An evergreen honeysuckle (*Lonicera henryi*) provides privacy, and also shelter for birds.

9.

Artist's garden
Blend nature with artistic expression to create a space that feels at once serene and stimulating.

This artistic garden balances structure, colour and texture with lush planting to create an intriguing outdoor retreat. The focal point is a red-painted feature wall with bespoke sculpted heads set into recessed niches. Like a painting, the colour palette should evoke emotion, and this warm hue of red brings energy to the space.

Texture is also key, and feathery ornamental grasses, sculptural succulents and smooth paving stones provide contrast and depth. The elevated dining area, accessed via a wooden deck, is positioned to best appreciate the talking-point sculptures. Glass brick screens flank the space, introducing a modern architectural touch while allowing light to pass through. These transparent partitions balance privacy with openness, softening the transition between the zones.

The planting is thoughtfully arranged to bring texture and further visual interest. The silvery tones of false dittany contrast with the structural forms of a potted striped mathiasella and the bold vertical lines of yellow iris. The airy qualities of the giant fennel and the pink geraniums add a layered dimension.

Create an artistic garden

Above *Mathiasella bupleuroides.*

Embrace a painter's palette

Use plants like pigments, selecting those that reflect a distinct visual style. You might channel the vibrancy of Van Gogh with gold black-eyed Susans (*Rudbeckia hirta*) and scarlet crocosmias, or lean into the softness of the Impressionists with pastel-coloured salvias, roses and silver-foliaged perennials.

Combine unusual, expressive plants

Choose plants with sculptural or eccentric character like *Mathiasella*, whose layered green bracts age beautifully into blush pink, or false dittany (*Ballota pseudodictamnus*), with its soft, silvery, trailing form. These function like brushstrokes: some calm and atmospheric, others unexpected.

Use garden objects like gallery pieces

Integrate sculpture, found materials or hand-thrown ceramics as focal points within the planting. Weathered stone, rusted metal or polished wood can act as both counterpoint and complement to natural textures. Place them as you would in an interior, framed by planting and visible from key sightlines.

Play with geometry and texture

Contrast is key: feathery grasses like Mexican feather grass (*Stipa tenuissima*) or airy fennel can soften the edges of strong forms such as alliums, upright iris or topiaries. Mixing soft and sharp elements creates a sense of movement and intentional composition. Groupings of plants punctuated by empty spaces can also evoke a minimalist or modernist aesthetic.

Shape the journey

A curved route adds romance and mystery, while angular paths reinforce a graphic look. Each step can frame a new view or draw attention to a detail, evoking the experience of walking through an exhibition. Arches and trellises can be used to highlight and frame focal points.

Experiment with unexpected materials

Use translucent or reflective surfaces like glass bricks or water to introduce light play and contrast. Weathered concrete, patinated copper or painted metal add graphic interest, reinforcing an intentional, curated aesthetic.

GARDEN FEATURES

(A) False dittany (*Ballota pseudodictamnus*), a compact shrub with silvery green leaves, thrives in sunny, dry spots.

(B) Geraniums provide soft ground cover with delicate pink blooms, introducing colour to the planting scheme.

(C) Vertical elements, including lilies, crocosmias and iris, add interest and contrast.

(D) Purple *Echeveria* is a sculptural succulent that thrives in containers.

(E) *Mathiasella* is known for its unique jade-green bracts that transition to pink, providing seasonal interest.

(F) Giant fennel (*Ferula communis*) is an airy umbellifer with tall, slender stems and fine foliage.

(G) The natural timber deck provides a smooth transition to the patio.

(H) Stone slabs offer durable and neutral paving that defines the dining area.

(I) A bold red feature wall anchors the space and highlights the niches that house the sculptures.

(J) Bespoke sculptures are artistic focal points, giving the garden its unique character.

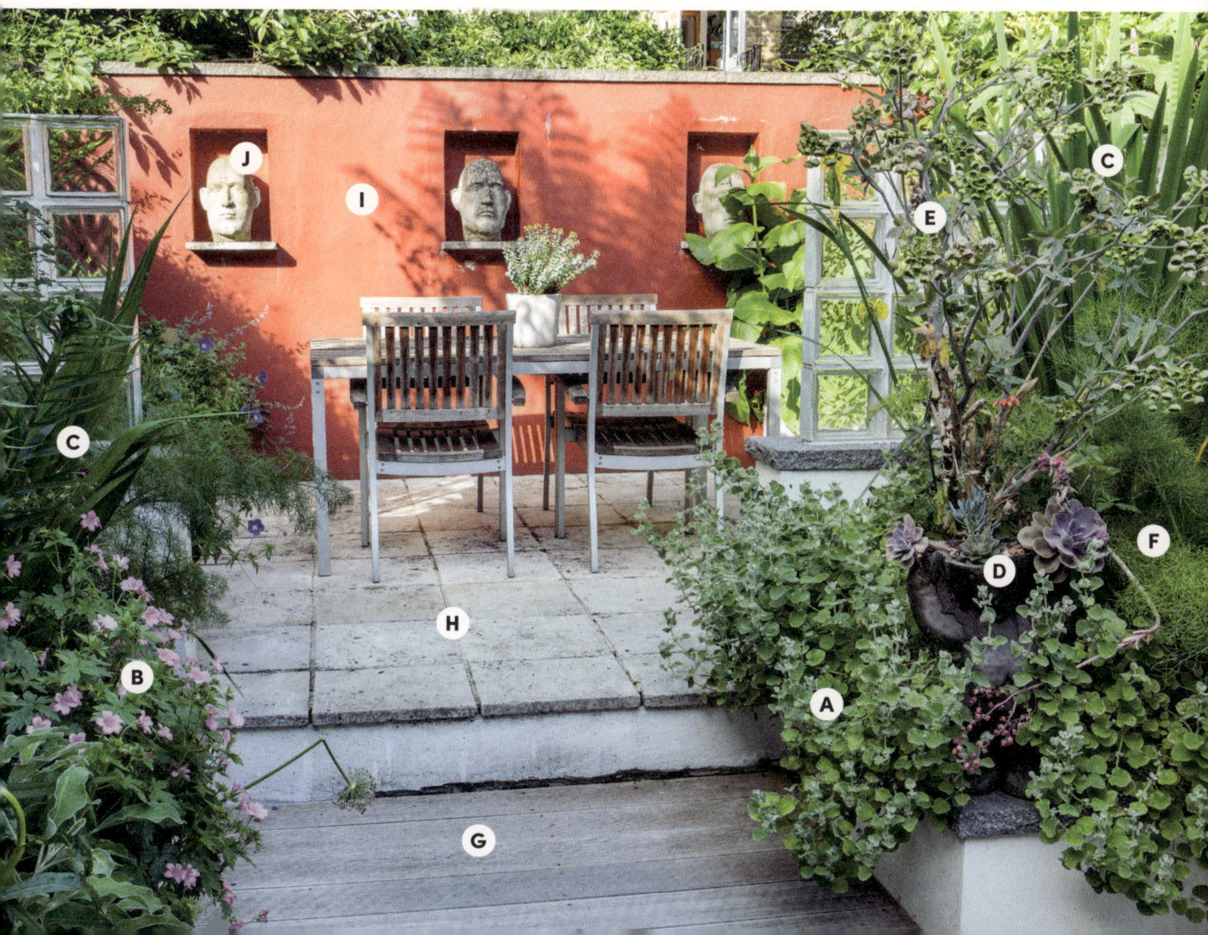

10.

Fire wheel

A fire pit adds warmth and atmosphere, creating a welcoming spot for relaxation and outdoor living.

A circular fire pit creates a natural focal point in the garden. It speaks to our most primal instincts, evoking a sense of safety and connection to nature. The flickering flames and crackling sounds create a comforting atmosphere, perfect for social gatherings, relaxation and fostering a simpler, more elemental outdoor experience.

This fire pit blends style with function and features integrated wood storage, providing both a sculptural centrepiece and a practical heating element for cooler evenings. Surrounding it is a custom-built wooden bench that offers generous integrated seating, allowing for ease of access around the fire.

A clever feature are the mulberry trees, which have been trained into flat umbrella canopies to create a natural pergola, filtering light and providing dappled shade. It's important to avoid positioning a fire close to any overhanging trees, so this is an ideal solution. Suspended rattan lanterns chime with the rustic vibe, the candles adding a soft glow, extending the garden's use into the evening while enhancing its cosy atmosphere.

A backdrop of multistemmed trees and lush planting frames the space, softening the structured lines and enriching the garden with texture and seasonal interest.

GARDEN FEATURES

- (A) The circular fireplace is both practical and a sculptural focal point.
- (B) A brick floor beneath the fire pit ensures durability and safety.
- (C) Custom-built wooden benches provide ample integrated seating.
- (D) Lanterns add an ambient glow, allowing the garden to be enjoyed into the evening.
- (E) Mulberry trees offer dappled shade. The cultivar *Morus nigra* 'Fruitless' does not produce fruit that would soil the patio, as regular cultivars or species do.
- (F) Multistemmed trees like this Tibetan cherry (*Prunus serrula*) add seasonal interest. Other suitable species are serviceberry (*Amelanchier*), pride of India (*Koelreuteria*) and the heavenly scented seven-son flower tree (*Heptacodium miconioides*).
- (G) Small shrubs with aromatic leaves like *Lavendula angustifolia* 'Hidcote Blue' and tree gamander (*Teucrium fruticans*) near the seating area introduce fragrance and texture, enriching the sensory experience.

Incorporate an outdoor fire pit

Create a dedicated seating zone
Built-in benches offer a space-efficient solution, their low, enclosed forms framing the fire pit. Wood slats or stone finishes link the seating to the surrounding materials.

Use sculptural contrast
A circular fire bowl offers a deliberate contrast to the linear elements of decking or fencing, introducing a sculptural focal point. Materials like rusted Corten steel or matte black metal age beautifully.

Anchor the fire pit
Place the fire pit on a base of stone, brick or concrete to protect nearby surfaces from radiant heat or stray embers. Here, it is set on a metal base, ensuring that the wooden decking is shielded from direct contact with heat.

Incorporate structural planting
Umbrella-trained trees or multistemmed shrubs provide architectural framing for the fire zone, offering shade by day and enclosure at night. Choose species that won't drop flammable debris like pine needles or dry seed heads into the fire area.

Engage the senses with planting
Surround the space with aromatic herbs such as rosemary, thyme or lavender. Their scented oils release in the warmth, enhancing the sensory atmosphere. These low-growing species also keep the planting open around the fire.

Fire safety considerations
→ Position the fire pit at a safe distance from flammable materials; maintain a clear, non-combustible zone around the fire area.
→ Check prevailing wind directions to avoid smoke being blown towards the house, seating area or in the direction of your neighbours.
→ Keep a lid, spark screen or extinguisher nearby when in use.
→ Ensure adequate ventilation if the garden is enclosed, and never use fire pits under overhanging structures unless specifically designed for this.
→ Choose natural wood or bioethanol, depending on local regulations and environmental considerations. Never burn treated or painted wood.

Left Tree gamander (*Teucrium fruticans*).

11.

Rainforest retreat
Lush greenery and dense foliage bring a tranquil, tropical atmosphere to this outdoor space.

This incredible souterrain garden transforms a compact outdoor space into a tropical sanctuary. What the garden lacks in ground space is made up for in clever layered planting. A carefully curated selection of large-leaved, mostly evergreen plants, cascading ferns and elegant bamboo creates the impression of a secluded jungle, where greenery envelops the space in rich texture.

The transition between indoors and outdoors is blurred, with glass flooring reflecting light, greenery, sun and clouds, and also mimicking the shimmer of water, creating a feeling of openness.

The soft grey flooring connects visually with the indoor elements, reinforcing the continuity between house and garden. Contemporary loungers with a zesty pop of yellow in the cushions offer a stylish place to relax, while lush tree ferns contribute to the dense, layered canopy. Against this verdant backdrop, a restrained materials palette ensures that the dramatic foliage remains the focal point, creating a tranquil space that invites rest and contemplation.

The few deciduous shrubs like the Japanese maple and the large-leaved angelica tree add a dramatic touch in autumn when their foliage changes from green to rich yellow and orange.

GARDEN FEATURES

Ⓐ Glass flooring enhances the sense of space, reflecting natural light.

Ⓑ Grey concrete extends from indoors, unifying the interior and exterior spaces.

Ⓒ Contemporary outdoor loungers provide a sophisticated note.

Ⓓ Tree ferns *(Dicksonia antarctica)* form a lower layer of the planting with their large, arching fronds.

Ⓔ Pink strawberry tree (*Arbutus unedo* 'Rubra') adds structure with its striking bark and delicate pink blooms.

Ⓕ Angelica tree (*Aralia elata)* introduces a bold, architectural element with distinctive, deeply lobed leaves.

Ⓖ Japanese maple (*Acer palmatum* 'Linearilobum') provides delicate texture, contrasting with the larger foliage.

Ⓗ Black bamboo (*Phyllostachys nigra*) complements the planting layers and remains easy to control thanks to a rhizome barrier.

Ⓘ Japanese loquat (*Eriobotrya japonica*) brings evergreen structure and seasonal interest with its large leaves and winter flowers.

Ⓙ Cherry laurel *(Prunus laurocerasus*) offers year-round dense greenery.

Above Chinese rice-paper plant (*Tetrapanax papyrifer*).

Above Princess tree (*Paulownia*).

Plants to create a tropical look

NAME	HEIGHT	SPECIAL FEATURES
Soft tree fern *(Dicksonia antarctica)*	Up to 3m (10ft)	Large, elegant fronds; tropical vibe; always keep the trunk moist.
Princess tree *(Paulownia)*	Up to 20m (60ft)	Large leaves; best pruned hard to the ground every two years for maximum sized leaves.
Chinese fountain bamboo (*Fargesia nitida*)	Up to 3m (10ft)	Clumping bamboo that is non-invasive, unlike the featured *Phyllostachys* species.
Oak-leaved hydrangea (*Hydrangea quercifolia*)	Up to 2.5m (8ft)	Oak leaf-shaped leaves with showy blooms; produces fiery autumn colour.
Chinese rice-paper plant (*Tetrapanax papyrifer*)	Up to 4m (13ft)	Large, deeply lobed leaves with an exotic look; spreads by runners.
Chinese windmill palm (*Trachycarpus fortunei*)	Up to 8m (26ft)	Fan-leaved palm for shade and semi-shade; keep away from strong winds.

You can immerse yourself in nature even if you live way above ground. Here are some ideas for edible gardens, sky-high entertaining spaces and dealing with exposed situations.

BALCONIES & ROOF TERRACES

1.

Rooftop haven
An enchanting space to relax perched above the bustling city streets.

When designing a small roof terrace, balance functionality with aesthetics by prioritizing space-saving furniture, lightweight materials and low-maintenance planting. Despite its openness, this design offers privacy through a combination of tall planters and evergeen shrubs along the railing, which block out noise and break gusts of wind. To ensure comfort across the day, a flexible shading, such as a freestanding parasol or retractable awning, can be used to manage exposure to sun or wind.

The floor is laid with brick tiles, introducing warm shades that are echoed in the wooden tabletop and chairs. Along the edges, a narrow strip of dark grey pebbles separates the walls from the brick floor, concealing the drainage. The walls, painted in a warm grey, include integrated planting beds filled with evergreen boxwood for year-round interest.

A metal planter in a matching dark grey houses a selection of perennials, while a zinc planter filled with succulents including echeverias and aeoniums as well as drought- and heat-tolerant perennials like ornamental asparagus, aloes and kangaroo's paws further reinforces the grey palette. A reclining chair, topped with soft grey upholstery, ties in neatly with the walls and pebbles, while pink and orange cushions complement the bright blooms.

Considerations for a tiny terrace

Less is more

A restrained palette of greys and warm earth tones creates harmony, while repeating materials across flooring, containers and furnishings unifies the design. Keeping forms simple allows plants and textures to take centre stage.

Easy-to-clean surfaces

Roof terraces are open to wind and rain, so surfaces must be durable and non-slip. Brick decking, metal planters and gravel all cope well with exposure and require little upkeep. Smooth yet porous materials offer both practicality and a comfortable underfoot feel.

Natural materials

Natural finishes such as timber, stone and galvanized metal soften the look of urban rooftops. Here, wooden chairs, zinc containers and pebbles create a tactile mix of tones and textures.

Low maintenance

Heat-tolerant, drought-resistant plants like succulents, ornamental grasses and Mediterranean herbs and perennials require minimal input. Opt for evergreen structure combined with seasonal flowering to maintain interest year-round. Self-watering or lightweight containers reduce workload and protect the rooftop structure. Consider an automatic irrigation system if you have a tap on the balcony.

Seasonal interest

Succulents such as aeoniums, echeverias and aloes provide structure, while flowering varieties like kangaroo's paw (*Anigozanthos*) inject seasonal colour. Use removable cushions or changeable pots to refresh the look throughout the year.

Privacy and comfort

Terraces are overlooked, so use planters, screens or rail-height hedging to shield the space while still letting in light. Strategic placement of tall grasses, shrubs or trellised climbers can muffle noise and add a sense of seclusion. An adjustable shade helps manage strong sun and wind without compromising the open-air feel.

Left Glaucus echeveria (*Echeveria secunda* f. *secunda*).

GARDEN FEATURES

(A) Brick paving lays a warm-toned foundation that complements the terrace's muted palette.

(B) Decorative vases in minimalist white add a sculptural accent.

(C) Zinc planters with perennials and succulents introduce a contemporary feel. On the left are asparagus, agaves and echeverias, with aeoniums, aloes and a jade plant (*Crassula ovata*) on the right.

(D) A reclining lounger blends in, while cushions add a pop of colour. Weatherproof and UV-resistant materials ensure furnishings can withstand exposure to the elements.

(E) Integrated planters filled with evergreen boxwood and perennials offer structure, privacy and year-round greenery.

(F) A space-saving foldable bistro set makes the space functional and is easily stowed.

(G) A pebble border in dark grey frames the decking, concealing the drainage.

(H) An automatic irrigation system (here with a drip hose) makes maintenance on balconies much easier.

2.

Sky garden

A tranquil garden room with panoramic vistas high above the city.

If you're lucky enough to have a rooftop terrace with a view, make the most of it as a luxurious entertaining space where you can sit and soak up the sunset. While this height offers exceptional views, it can get pretty blowy, and this design incorporates features to counteract this, with windbreak plantings and heavy-based furniture.

The floor is laid with warm-toned wooden decking, introducing a natural texture that contrasts with the crisp light beige lounge furniture. Large, deep grey planters define the edges, filled with a striking mix of architectural succulents, grasses and evergreen shrubs like oleander and Mediterranean dwarf palm that provide structure and movement.

Generous seating fills the space, but is upholstered in light colours so does not feel overpowering. Around the perimeter, integrated lighting illuminates the planting, enhancing the terrace's ambiance as day transitions to night. The carefully curated palette of muted greys, warm wood and greens is elevated by the golden light reflecting off the foliage.

The high planters with wind-resistant plants shield the seating areas from gusts and create the illusion of a private, sunken garden. Even though there is not much risk of curious onlookers at this height, this setting feels far more comfortable and secluded.

GARDEN FEATURES

- (A) Neutral lounge furniture in weather-resistant fabric fits neatly into the space. Use furniture with weighted bases to keep it stable and reduce the risk of being blown around.
- (B) A wooden deck with a grey patina provides warmth and texture.
- (C) Dark grey planters define the space. Using tall, dense plants like ornamental grasses and evergreen shrubs in large planters helps to create a natural barrier.
- (D) Grasses with a maritime look (see opposite) visually connect the terrace with the river view, adding movement and softness.
- (E) Structural plants such as agaves create striking focal points, their bold forms highlighted by spotlights.
- (F) Evergreen oleander offers privacy and acts as a windbreak, enhancing comfort in the exposed rooftop setting.
- (G) Mediterranean dwarf palms (*Chamaerops humilis*) tolerate heat and drought, making them a better fit for the space than windmill palms.
- (H) Mediterranean semi-shrubs like lavender, thyme, sage and rosemary add fragrance and texture and thrive in the extreme rooftop conditions.

Above *Agave desmetiana* 'Variegata'.

Perfect plants for windy roof terraces

GROUP	HEIGHT	SUITABLE SPECIES
Perennials and semi-shrubs	Up to 1m (3¼ft)	Lavender, thyme, sage, rosemary, stonecrop (*Sedum* spp.), verbena
Mediterranean and exotic shrubs	Up to 2.5m (8¼ft)	Oleander, olive trees, fig trees, pomegranate, boxwood, Portuguese laurel (*Prunus lusitanica*)
Grasses	Up to 2m (6½ft)	Chinese silver grass (*Miscanthus sinensis*), fountain grass (*Pennisetum alopecuroides*), marram grass (*Ammophila arenaria*), switchgrass (*Panicum virgatum*), Mexican feather grass (*Stipa tenuissima*)
Palms	Up to 2m (6½ft)	Mediterranean dwarf palm (*Chamaerops humilis*), Phoenix palm (*Phoenix dactylifera*)
Climbers	Up to 5m (16½ft)	Clematis, grapevine (*Vitis vinifera*), trumpet vine (*Campsis radicans*), wisteria, honeysuckle (*Lonicera* spp.), Virginia creeper (*Parthenocissus quinquefolia*)

3.

Edible balcony

A rooptop kitchen garden with beds of herbs, vegetables and edible flowers.

This urban rooftop terrace shows how a small space can be turned into a bountiful kitchen garden. Raised wooden planters are filled with aromatic herbs and edible greenery to create a layered display that looks and smells great and is productive, too. The planting scheme is naturalistic, integrating culinary staples like sage, oregano and thyme with structural plants like silvery senecio and the bold foliage of borage.

The warm wood and dark metal in the balcony's protective railing contrasts with the greenery and connects with the cityscape. Plants have been chosen to thrive in these sunny to semi-shade conditions, and their ability to adapt makes them perfect for a rooftop garden. Beyond the planters of herbs and vegetables, ornamental beds are filled with roses and edible flowers like calendulas.

For herbs and compact vegetables, planters should be at least 20–30cm (8–12in) deep to allow adequate root growth. Lightweight materials such as wood, zinc or fibreglass reduce strain on rooftop structures (consult an engineer when installing larger containers or raised beds as they can become quite heavy, especially when filled and watered to capacity).

Railing planters or vertical systems are ideal for tight balconies like this. Use these for trailing herbs like thyme, compact salad greens or edible flowers. Grouping plants by watering needs also makes care easier and reduces stress on the plants.

Above Sage (*Salvia officinalis*).

Above Chives (*Allium schoenoprasum*).

Successful container herbs

GROUP	WATER REQUIREMENTS	SUITABLE SPECIES
Kitchen herbs	Medium	Parsley, chives, coriander, dill, lovage, tarragon
Mediterranean herbs	Low	Lavender, thyme, sage, rosemary, hyssop, oregano
Tea herbs	Medium–low	Lemon balm, chamomile, mint, aniseed, fennel, calendula
Microgreens	Medium	Mustard greens, radish greens, cress, sunflower shoots, pea greens
Salad	Medium	Asian greens, rocket (arugula), leaf lettuce, lamb's lettuce
Aromatic plants (non-edible)	Medium	Russian sage (*Perovskia*), curry plant (*Helichrysum italicum*), catmint (*Nepeta*), lavender cotton (*Santolina chamaecyparissus*)

GARDEN FEATURES

Ⓐ A see-through railing provides safety while keeping the space open and visually connected to the surroundings.

Ⓑ Sage offers fragrant, velvety foliage and a robust flavour. Here two varieties are used: 'Icterina' with yellow-green mottled leaves and 'Purpurascens' with purplish foliage.

Ⓒ Oregano brings a Mediterranean touch, thriving in the well-drained, sunlit conditions of the raised beds.

Ⓓ Chives add height and texture with their slender green stems and delicate purple flowers. For variety, plant cultivars with white flowers like 'Elbe' or 'Corsican White'.

Ⓔ Thyme spreads between other herbs, forming a fragrant ground cover that attracts pollinators.

Ⓕ Dusty miller (*Senecio cineraria*) contributes silvery foliage. Note: This plant is not edible, but provides contrast and year-round structure.

Ⓖ Borage stands out with its large, textured leaves and vibrant blue edible flowers, beloved by bees.

Urban prairie

Ornamental perennials and grasses create a wildlife garden in the heart of the city.

This rooftop prairie garden uses native grasses, wildflowers and perennials that thrive in the local conditions and attract bees, butterflies and birds, making it a hotbed of biodiversity. Once established, it requires minimal upkeep and provides year-round interest. The design embraces naturalistic planting, blending soft pinks and lilacs with ornamental grasses to create a light, airy feel. The drought-tolerant perennials and grasses intermingle in an ever-changing display of texture and movement.

Natural materials such as wooden shingles are used in the hardscaping, which discreetly conceals essential yet unattractive structures. The warm, natural hues complement the wooden bench and decking and the earthy tones of the surrounding brickwork, fostering a sense of organic visual harmony. Custom-built integrated planters and a wooden bench provide space to sit, and allow enough room for the deep roots of the planting.

The terrace is enclosed by a transparent railing with netting, ensuring visual openness while providing security. The pop of orange echoes the brick facades of nearby buildings. As the seasons transition, the garden undergoes a metamorphosis, and during the late summer months it is graced with a haze of pink yarrow, stonecrop, verbenas and grasses that sway in the breeze.

Create a layered planting

A prairie-inspired planting scheme brings softness and movement to hard-edged rooftops or balconies. The key is combining structure and spontaneity.

Height and seasonal rhythm

Start by establishing a vertical framework using upright grasses such as feather reed grass. These act as gentle screens, introduce movement in the wind and catch the light. Pair these with mid-height, pollinator-friendly perennials like yarrow (*Achillea*), stonecrop (*Hylotelephium spectabile*), salvias or verbenas to add weight and colour during the growing season.

Low-growing species such as catmint (*Nepeta*), cranesbill (*Geranium* 'Rozanne') or thyme weave through the base, softening the edges of the planters. Interplanting ensures a long visual season and a tapestry of texture that changes through the year.

Avoid symmetry

Instead of planting in rows or rigid blocks, stagger your plants in naturalistic groupings. Allow one species to drift into the next, use odd numbers and vary the spacing to create rhythm.

Deep planters

Grasses and long-lived perennials thrive in containers at least 40–60cm (1½–2ft) deep, with good drainage and water retention. Modular raised beds or custom-built timber planters help insulate roots against heat and wind. Opt for lightweight substrates mixed with mineral aggregates and water-retentive layers such as coir.

Above Feather reed grass (*Calamagrostis × acutiflora* 'Karl Foerster').

Pairings for different conditions

→ **Full sun:** feather grass (*Stipa*), purple top (*Verbena bonariensis*), sea holly (*Eryngium*), gaura (*Oenothera lindheimeri*), yarrow (*Achillea*)

→ **Part-shade:** cranesbill (*Geranium macrorrhizum*), sedges (*Carex morrowii*), Siberian bugloss (*Brunnera macrophylla*), columbine (*Aquilegia*)

→ **Exposed or windy sites:** catmint (*Nepeta*), yarrow (*Achillea*) and scabious (*Scabiosa*), which sway without snapping

Planting for wildlife

Choose nectar-rich flowers with long blooming periods to support biodiversity. In addition to the above, plants such as salvias, coneflower (*Echinacea*) and Mediterranean scabious (*Knautia*) attract bees, while grasses left uncut over winter offer shelter and seeds for small birds. If space allows, add a shallow water bowl.

GARDEN FEATURES

Ⓐ Wooden shingles disguise functional structures.

Ⓑ Custom-built wooden bench with room for root growth of the plants.

Ⓒ Wooden decking enhances the natural, organic feel of the space.

Ⓓ The transparent railing with added netting adds safety without obstructing the surrounding views.

Ⓔ Stonecrop (*Hylotelephium spectabile*) brings late-season colour with its dusky pink blooms that attract pollinators.

Ⓕ Yarrow (*Achillea)* – here a pink form – provides delicate, flat-topped flowers, adding structure.

Ⓖ Grasses introduce movement and texture, enhancing the prairie-inspired aesthetic.

Ⓗ Balkan clary (*Salvia nemorosa)*, with its upright spires of purple flowers, contrasts with the umbrella-shaped flowers of the stonecrops and yarrows.

Ⓘ American blue vervain (*Verbena hastata*) has long-lasting spikes of small violet-blue to pinkish-purple flowers on tall, branched stems from early summer to early autumn.

5.

Sunny terrace
Drought-tolerant plants are ideal for roof terraces that receive a lot of sunshine.

This rooftop terrace is designed to show off the natural beauty of plants that can tolerate dry conditions. The design takes inspiration from wild meadows, balancing structure with softness through a carefully selected range of perennials and ornamental grasses.

Using a simple palette of materials makes the space feel light and airy. Pale wood for decking, pergolas and railings give it a warm feel, as opposed to the cooler atmosphere created by the use of grey metal or concrete, and complement the soft colours of the plants. Gravel underfoot not only helps with drainage but also adds texture to the natural look, creating a smooth transition between hard and soft landscaping.

Tall purple top stands out with its airy flowers, set against the soft Chinese feather grass and the bright colours of pheasant's tail grass. Lower-growing perennials like yarrow and alum root add layers of colour and texture, while fountain grass cultivars bring in rich red and bronze tones that deepen as the seasons change. All these elements come together to create a space that feels natural, filled with movement and light.

Create a drought-resistant roof garden

Gravel is ideal for rooftop gardens, where weight, water retention and exposure must be carefully managed. It requires minimal upkeep, and offers exceptional resilience to drought.

Gravel selection

Choose angular gravel (rather than rounded pebbles), as it locks into place and provides a stable surface. A particle size of 6–10mm (¼–⅜in) is ideal – large enough to allow water to drain freely, but fine enough to support delicate stems. Avoid very pale gravels, which reflect light harshly; instead use mid-grey or honey-toned options.

Layered soil and gravel mix

A well-draining substrate is essential. Start with a lightweight base layer using a mix of expanded clay aggregate, lava rock or pumice to reduce overall weight. Above this, use a soil mix consisting of 40% loam, 30% sharp sand or grit and 30% well-rotted compost or other organic matter like leaf mould. Top-dress with 3–5cm (1–2in) of gravel to suppress weeds, prevent evaporation and create a clean finish.

Irrigation and drainage

Good drainage is non-negotiable on rooftops. Raised beds or containers should include perforated bases or integrated drainage pipes. Infrequent, deep watering is preferable to regular surface sprinkling. Drip irrigation systems offer efficient, low-tech watering options.

Maintenance

Once established, gravel gardens require minimal input. Occasional weeding in the first season, light pruning to shape and cutting back grasses in late winter are often all that's needed. Apply a slow-release fertilizer once in spring for sustained growth without overstimulation.

Above Fountain grass (*Pennisetum alopecuroides*).

Complementary hardscaping

Pair gravel with clean-lined timber decking or Corten steel edging to create warm material contrasts. Use upright elements like slim pergolas, sculptural containers or metal plant supports to add height and rhythm without too much extra weight.

Plant pairings

In addition to the plantings shown in this garden, consider the following resilient combinations:

- → **Fountain grass (*Pennisetum alopecuroides* 'Little Bunny'):** a compact grass thriving in full sun.
- → **Rock rose (*Cistus × purpureus*):** evergreen, drought-tolerant and long flowering.
- → **Snow-in-summer (*Cerastium tomentosum*):** silver foliage and white blooms for ground cover.
- → **Horehound (*Marrubium vulgare*):** soft, woolly texture and low-spreading habit.
- → **Thyme (*Thymus*):** aromatic herb with pink flowers.

GARDEN FEATURES

Ⓐ Purple top (*Verbena bonariensis*) provides height and a delicate, floating effect with its purple blooms.

Ⓑ Chinese feather grass (*Miscanthus* 'Gracillimus') adds soft, arching foliage that sways in the wind. This cultivar flowers only in very warm years and is mainly used for its airy and elegant foliage.

Ⓒ Pheasant's tail grass (*Anemanthele lessoniana*) introduces warm golden tones that intensify through the seasons.

Ⓓ Yarrow (*Achillea*) contributes a flat-topped floral structure in shades of pink, attracting pollinators.

Ⓔ Dark bronze-coloured alum root (*Heuchera*) offers contrasting foliage and year-round interest.

Ⓕ Red-leaved forms of *Pennisetum* such as 'Rubrum' or 'Fireworks' introduce deep, rich hues and movement.

Ⓖ Light wooden structures like pergolas or railings provide vertical interest and define the space while maintaining an open feel. The usable space was deliberately reduced here in favour of space for plants.

Ⓗ Pale wood decking gives a warm and natural feel.

Private sanctuary

Create a feeling of calm seclusion with carefully chosen greenery.

This urban terrace faces an inner courtyard garden flanked with mature trees, so it feels like a private retreat in the midst of a busy neighbourhood. It shows how greenery can soften hard lines, create privacy and make outdoor living more relaxing, even in a built-up area.

The materials palette mixes natural elements with modern. A glass screen encloses the seating area without concealing the view of the lush greenery beyond the terrace, which makes the space feel bigger than it actually is. The dark grey planters and woven furniture add to the sophisticated yet relaxed feel, and the seating is arranged to best appreciate the view across the garden.

The planting scheme features ornamental grasses and lavender, chosen for their movement, texture and resilience in an urban setting. The soft forms of Mexican feather grass catch the light and sway in the breeze, while fragrant lavender adds seasonal interest and attracts pollinators. Flowering trees, such as false acacias, shield the space from surrounding buildings and act as a buffer to help reduce noise.

GARDEN FEATURES

(A) An integrated fireplace extends the usability of the terrace into cooler months.

(B) Woven furniture introduces a soft, textural contrast to the hard materials of the terrace.

(C) Transparent screen separates the seating area from the planting while maintaining an open feel, giving the illusion of space.

(D) Mexican feather grass (*Stipa tenuissima*) provides movement, texture and fragrance. Fescue grasses like *Festuca glauca*, with its bluish leaves, is an alternative for more subtle colour.

(E) Lavender is ideal for dry, sunny balconies. The fragrant leaves and flowers develop their best aroma when fertilizer and water are kept to a minimum.

(F) Flowering trees like false acacia (*Robinia*) create a natural screen from neighbouring buildings, offering privacy and seasonal interest.

(G) Heat and drought-resilient plants like fleabane (*Erigeron*) are also low-maintenance.

(H) Raised planters provide a structured base for planting, anchoring the design.

Create privacy with plants

Colour palette

The colour green is scientifically proven to soothe the senses and encourage relaxation. A carefully selected palette of greenery can soften hard urban lines, absorb noise and create a calming atmosphere.

Seasonal considerations

Mix evergreens with deciduous shrubs and trees to balance year-round structure with seasonal variety. Evergreens provide a stable, green backbone, ensuring privacy even in winter, while deciduous species introduce dynamic interest through blossoms, autumn colour and shifting leaf textures.

Maximize growth

Apply the 'right plant, right place' concept to ensure species thrive in their given conditions. Assessing factors such as sun exposure, wind patterns and soil type is key to selecting plants that will establish well and require minimal care. Choose heat- and wind-tolerant species for challenging rooftop or courtyard environments.

Clever hardscaping

Combine elements like glass screens and trellises with plants to create layered privacy without compromising on light and openness. Transparent or frosted glass panels, when paired with grasses, shrubs or small trees, offer a balance between enclosure and visibility.

Top Lavender (*Lavendula angustifolia*).
Bottom Mexican feather grass (*Stipa tenuissima*).

7.

A roof with a view
This urban oasis balances resilience and beauty in the exposed conditions of a sky-high terrace.

With amazing views over the city and enjoying an abundance of golden evening light, this is a visually stunning outdoor space. However, full sun exposure comes with challenges like intense heat and rapid water evaporation, making this a tough environment for many plants. This rooftop terrace blends smart design with lush, drought-tolerant species.

A weathered wooden deck forms the base of the design, its silvery effect echoing the tones of the city skyline. The natural textures of wood and woven material in the outdoor dining set bring warmth and comfort. Large dark grey planters anchor the planting scheme, allowing a mix of Mediterranean and steppe-style species to thrive in the challenging rooftop conditions.

A key feature of this terrace is the use of wind-resistant plants, including Mediterranean dwarf palms, pines and perennials that endure the heat and exposure of high-altitude settings. Bold architectural forms, such as New Zealand flax, add structure, while flowering perennials like Balkan clary introduce seasonal interest. The planting extends to the terrace's edge, where a transparent railing ensures unobstructed views.

Make the most of exposed rooftops

Rooftop gardens are exposed to the full force of sun and wind, so it's important to factor this into the design.

Durable materials

Opt for surfaces and furnishings that age gracefully and resist wear. Hardwood decking develops a soft silver patina over time, while powder-coated metal or woven resin furniture withstands sun and rain without deterioration.

Wind-tolerant planting

Mediterranean dwarf palms (*Chamaerops humilis*) are more wind-resistant than traditional windmill palms. Perennials such as Balkan clary (*Salvia nemorosa*), New Zealand flax (*Phormium*) and grasses provide vertical movement without fragility, while bamboo is best used in more sheltered roof gardens or alongside screens.

Use generous containers

Large planters help stabilize tall plants and prevent them from drying out too quickly. They also protect roots from extreme heat or frost. Use lightweight, frost resistant materials like fibre cement or reinforced resin to reduce weight without compromising on size.

Create shade and shelter

Incorporate architectural elements like pergolas or canopies, or rely on tall plants and trees to offer natural shelter and shade. Conifers and pines adapted to mountainous climates are particularly suited to rooftop conditions.

Above *Allium* 'Globemaster'.

Blur the boundaries

Let planting reach the edges to visually merge the garden with the horizon. When pots line the parapet and spill over the boundary, the eye travels through planting rather than stopping at the edge, so you feel immersed in greenery, even above the city skyline.

Plan for access and water

Install irrigation early – drip systems are ideal – or position taps nearby. Make sure furniture is lightweight or modular so it can be moved easily, and consider how plants and materials will be delivered and maintained on site.

GARDEN FEATURES

Ⓐ The silvered decking harmonizes with the tones of the city skyline.

Ⓑ Wooden outdoor dining furniture with woven seating is durable.

Ⓒ Dark grey containers provide a uniform base for the planting scheme.

Ⓓ Mediterranean dwarf palms (*Chamaerops humilis*) withstand heat and wind well.

Ⓔ Perennials like Balkan clary (*Salvia nemorosa*) offer many blooms through the seasons.

Ⓕ Grasses and sword-like foliage plants, including New Zealand flax (*Phormium*), thrive in windy conditions.

Ⓖ Bamboo is best suited to wind-sheltered areas in partial shade, adding height and screening. Use clump-forming *Fargesia* as they are less aggressive than *Phyllostachys* species.

Ⓗ Conifers from dry or mountainous regions, such as pines, are well-adapted to the exposed rooftop conditions.

Ⓘ A transparent railing maintains unobstructed views while ensuring safety.

Ⓙ *Allium* 'Globemaster' is a bulbous perennial with large pink flower heads in early summer that keep their shape until late winter.

These designs embrace nature's flow, focusing on loose drifts of planting and natural materials. Perfect for cottage-style or wildlife-friendly gardens, they encourage spontaneity and charm over structure and precision.

INFORMAL & NATURAL GARDENS

1.

Cottage corner

Vibrant colours, varied textures and layered plantings transform a small, shady corner.

This small garden makes a big impact through bold planting. In a tiny corner plot like this, every plant matters. Here we see varieties that work well together and bloom at different times to keep the garden looking fresh year-round. This thoughtful layering of evergreen structure and seasonal blooms provides continual colour and greenery.

To make the space seem larger, taller plants are layered at the back and mid-sized flowers in the middle, while ground cover at the front creates depth. The white garden walls create a bright backdrop for evergreens like wintercreeper and tawhiwhi, which add structure and interest throughout the year, their glossy leaves gently spilling down the walls.

At ground level, dark-leaved mondo grass and bronze-coloured alum root provide pockets of inky foliage, creating focal points along the path. The bright blooms of rose campion, among others, pop against the darker tones, providing a playful accent that draws the eye.

Lush foliage in purple-bronze shades contrasts with the light-coloured gravel path, which leads to a compact oak bench. Framed by densely planted perennials and flowers, the bench feels as though it is tucked away, offering a quiet spot to pause and enjoy the view.

GARDEN FEATURES

(A) A structured, flat stone terrace offers a stable, elegant surface.

(B) The textured gravel path introduces a tactile and auditory dimension and allows for rainwater drainage.

(C) A bespoke oak bench provides a quiet vantage point to view the garden.

(D) Climbers like wintercreeper (*Euonymus fortunei*) and tawhiwhi (*Pittosporum tenuifolium* 'Tom Thumb'), and trained shrubs like lilacs (*Syringa*) and shrub roses soften the walls, adding vertical interest, seasonal variation and a habitat for wildlife.

(E) A mix of perennials and bedding plants like rose campion (*Lychnis coronaria*), lady's mantle (*Alchemilla mollis*), delphinium, cosmos, crocosmias, daisies and elephant's ears (*Bergenia*) enriches the garden with seasonal colour and enhances biodiversity.

(F) The deep, almost black, foliage of mondo grass (*Ophiopogon planiscapus* 'Nigrescens') and alum root (*Heuchera*) create a striking contrast against lighter gravel and pavings while adding texture.

(G) A diverse planting palette supports ecological balance, fostering a thriving microhabitat.

Planting solutions for small corners

Open surfaces

Instead of a lawn, which may struggle in shaded conditions, opt for well-defined planting beds, gravel paths or permeable surfaces to enhance drainage. Since shady corners can be dark and cool, use contrast and texture to make the space feel alive.

Mixed plantings

A diverse and irregular planting scheme helps replicate nature. Combining a variety of species ensures interest while reducing the risk of gaps should plants fail. Layering textures, heights and colours will create a sense of depth, making the space feel more immersive.

Privacy

A well-designed corner garden should feel like a secluded retreat. Tall grasses, dense shrubs and evergreen hedging help create a sense of enclosure. If your garden is overlooked, vertical screens or trellises with climbing plants can further block unwanted views and help define the space.

Climbers and espaliers

When floor space is limited, vertical planting offers a solution. Espaliered trees, which are trained to grow flat against a wall, trellised climbers and slender columnar shrubs provide greenery without encroaching on pathways or seating areas.

Above Alum root (*Heuchera*).

Seasonal interest

Combine evergreen planting with species that offer seasonal variation. Aside from those included here, good options include shrubs like Portuguese laurel (*Prunus lusitanica*) to provide a permanent green framework, while flowering perennials such as cranesbill (*Geranium* 'Rozanne'), Balkan clary (*Salvia nemorosa*) and purple coneflower (*Echinacea purpurea*) introduce colour through spring and summer. Fruit-bearing plants like crab apple (*Malus* 'Evereste') or blueberry offer spring blossom and fruit in late summer and autumn. For vivid autumn foliage, incorporate small trees or shrubs. Ground covers like bugleweed (*Ajuga reptans*) and barrenwort (*Epimedium* × *perralchicum*) ensure the space stays lush even in winter.

2.

Shaded woodland
Low-maintenance, unstructured beauty using shade-tolerant plants and natural textures.

Shaded areas often pose a challenge for traditional grass lawns, which need sunlight and frequent care. Gravel, however, offers a practical alternative that suits these conditions perfectly, providing a durable, low-maintenance ground cover. In this garden the gravel beds host a mix of shade-tolerant London pride, grasses, ferns, umbrella plant and rodgersias. When in bloom, the London pride's delicate pinkish-white flowers lend an airy, ephemeral feel.

Incorporating elements like wooden borders, stepping stones and seating areas helps break up the space and provides focal points within the gravel area. Graphic diagonal designs on one fence (see over the page) adds a modern twist, and a wooden table and benches sit on stone pavers, providing a relaxed area for alfresco meals.

A sleek stone bench at the rear of the garden supports a collection of rare alpine plants, herbs and small shrubs that thrive in terracotta pots, bringing variety in colour and form. This mix of loose, textural planting and light-coloured gravel helps the garden feel balanced, with a soft, natural feel. The result is a tranquil retreat that embraces both wild beauty and clean-lined design.

Ideas for shaded gardens

Perennials for shade

Select plants that naturally thrive in low light to create a textured display. Reliable choices include lady's mantle (*Alchemilla mollis*) with its frothy lime flowers, Japanese anemone (*Anemone hupehensis*) for late-summer blooms, foam flower (*Tiarella cordifolia*) for ground cover and Solomon's seal (*Polygonatum odoratum*) for graceful arching stems. Taller options like foxgloves (*Digitalis purpurea*) and rodgersia add height and dramatic foliage.

Selecting gravel

Choose gravel in soft neutral tones such as light grey, buff or honeyed beige to reflect light into shady corners and make the area feel brighter. A finer grade is more comfortable underfoot, while coarser gravel offers a rugged, informal aesthetic. Mix different grades subtly for added texture.

Softening gravel edges

Soften transitions between hard surfaces and planting with mounding ground covers like sweet woodruff (*Galium odoratum*), barrenwort (*Epimedium × perralchicum*) or lilyturf (*Liriope muscari*). Their low, flowing shapes break up straight lines, helping the gravel to feel integrated into the planting.

Maintaining gravel surfaces

Installing a permeable membrane beneath the gravel is asking for trouble as the roots of weeds will grow into and under it over time, making weeding almost impossible. To keep gravel paths neat, maintenance can be reduced by frequent light weeding. Regular raking keeps the surface evenly distributed. Top up thin areas with fresh gravel every couple of years.

Designing with structure

Use broad, durable elements like concrete paving slabs to anchor seating zones, and divide space with clear pathways edged by lush borders. Introduce focal points to draw the eye across the garden, and surround each focal point with tiered planting: lower-growing ground covers around the base, with mid-height shrubs and taller shrubs or small trees as vertical accents.

Left Foxglove (*Digitalis purpurea*).

GARDEN FEATURES

(A) Concrete slabs for the seating area provide a durable foundation.

(B) A modern wooden bench and table offer a focal point for outdoor dining.

(C) Gravel paths allow easy access while acting as mineral mulch for the planting.

(D) A privacy screen in warm brown and grey defines the space, with a concrete bench for terracotta potted plants.

(E) A hidden storage hut blends with the wooden boundary, maintaining the garden's clean lines.

(F) Ephemeral perennials like London pride (*Saxifraga* × *urbium*) bring lightness and seasonal charm.

(G) Tall shrubs like hydrangeas provide vertical interest.

(H) Lush grasses add softness and movement, with sedges (*Carex)* thriving in shade. Here, the golden weeping sedge (*Carex oshimensis* 'Everillo') is used in various parts of the garden to create rhythm in between the flowering perennials.

(I) Large-leaved perennials such as umbrella plants (*Darmera peltata*) and rodgersia provide bold contrast in shaded areas.

3.

Fern glen

Walking through cool, feathery undergrowth makes the entrance to this house feel like a special adventure.

Meandering down this shaded garden path feels like entering another world, one where nature takes centre stage and architecture is softened by a veil of lush greenery. Towering tree ferns with feathery fronds create a cool, enveloping canopy, while layers of hardy ferns and shade-loving evergreens provide texture. A climbing hydrangea clambers over the walls and a grapevine drapes over the brick arch, making a striking contrast to the weathered masonry.

Upright varieties of ferns are mixed with more delicate low-growing types, their different textures and colours adding depth to the space. Arranging the plants in clusters and layering them by height helps mimic how they would grow in the wild, enhancing the natural, organic feel of the garden.

At ground level, a tapestry of bellflowers and other ground covers spills along the path, adding softness and seasonal colour. Mature shrubs like boxwood and sweet box add evergreen structure, which makes the whole area feel enclosed. An old, ornamental metal gate and decorative accents such as mounted sculptural planters contribute to the garden's charming, timeless atmosphere.

GARDEN FEATURES

Ⓐ A tree fern forms the backbone of the planting scheme, its fronds creating height and drama.

Ⓑ Male ferns thrive in deep shade, their finely cut foliage adding texture beneath taller plants.

Ⓒ Evergreen shrubs such as boxwood (*Buxus sempervirens*), sweet box (*Sarcococca*) and Oregon grape (*Mahonia*) provide year-round structure and contrast with the soft ferns.

Ⓓ A climbing hydrangea (*Hydrangea petiolaris*) covers the border walls, softening them with seasonal blooms.

Ⓔ Bellflowers (*Campanula*) as ground cover fill gaps between stones, bringing delicate flowers to the shaded setting.

Ⓕ The old stone arch enhances the garden's character, adding a historic feel.

Ⓖ A rusted gate contributes to the sense of mystery, blending into the aged surroundings.

Ⓗ Near the house, clay pots hold classic bedding plants like pelargoniums and petunias which add a pop of colour among the greenery.

Above Male fern (*Dryopteris filix-mas*).

Above Japanese painted fern (*Athyrium niponicum*).

Top five ferns for shaded gardens

NAME	HEIGHT/SPREAD	SPECIAL FEATURES
Soft tree fern (*Dicksonia antarctica*)	Up to 4m/2.5m (13ft/8ft)	Striking architectural form, large elegant fronds.
Male fern (*Dryopteris filix-mas*)	1–2m/1–2m (3–6½ft/3–6½ft)	Hardy, robust, deep-green finely cut foliage.
Hart's tongue fern (*Asplenium scolopendrium*)	30–60cm/30–60cm (12–24in/12–24in)	Glossy, evergreen, strap-shaped fronds.
Soft shield fern (*Polystichum setiferum*)	60–90cm/45–90cm (24–35in/18–35in)	Finely divided, soft-textured fronds.
Japanese painted fern (*Athyrium niponicum*)	30–60cm/30–60cm (12–24in/12–24in)	Silvery foliage with purple veins, highly decorative.

4.

Jungle den
This verdant garden was transformed from a neglected storage space into a courtyard filled with life.

Formerly an uninviting utility space, this small urban courtyard has been transformed into a leafy sanctuary. Once used for refuse storage, it is now a lush retreat defined by dense, evergreen planting with a strong sense of enclosure. Surrounded by the shelter of buildings, this shaded space benefits from a stable microclimate, ideal for growing subtropical and broad-leaved evergreens that might struggle elsewhere in temperate regions.

Planting is layered to maximize vertical interest. Structural shrubs such as mock privet and climbers like rambling roses form a green canopy overhead, while pittosporum, hardy fig and broad-leaved bamboo add texture and mass at eye level. Beneath them, tropical-style plants such as ginger, African lily and salvia introduce colour and softness.

All planting is kept to the edges in raised beds or containers, leaving the central space free for a large teak table – an elegant contrast with the luxuriant greenery. Cool grey tones in the paving and furniture allow the varied greens and occasional blues and purples to stand out, especially in the evening light.

Planting ideas for shady courtyards

Plants follow place

Always choose species that suit the conditions of your site. Urban courtyards often have a milder microclimate than surrounding open spaces, thanks to heat retention in walls and shelter from wind. This makes it possible to grow plants with a subtropical appearance, even in temperate regions.

Foliage takes the lead

In shade, flowers tend to fade quickly or struggle, so the emphasis should be on leaf shape, size and colour. Use bold architectural foliage such as broad-leaved bamboo (*Sasa palmata*), fig (*Ficus carica*) or Chinese rice-paper plant (*Tetrapanax papyrifer*), complemented with the softer textures of ferns, hostas or elephant's ears (*Bergenia*).

Structure through evergreens

Reliable evergreen shrubs are key in small spaces. Mock privet (*Phillyrea*), pittosporum and spindle (*Euonymus*) provide volume, screen views, and maintain structure throughout the year. They also create a permanent framework for the planting scheme.

Design in layers

To build depth, structure planting in three layers: small trees or tall shrubs like mock privet, fig or loquat (*Eriobotrya japonica*) form the upper tier; medium-height foliage plants such as ginger, Japanese aralia (*Fatsia japonica*) or broad-leaved bamboo fill the space at eye level; and robust ground covers like elephant's ears, lilyturf (*Liriope muscari*) or barrenwort (*Epimedium × perralchicum*) knit the planting together at the base.

Above Ginger lily (*Hedychium densiflorum*).

Raised beds and edge planting

In small spaces, raised planters are essential. Position them around the perimeter to keep the central area open. This maximizes planting density while preserving usable space.

Use subtle colour

In low-light conditions, avoid complex colour schemes. Instead, choose a restrained palette of greens punctuated with cool hues such as white, blue and violet. These tones are especially effective in the evening, when the human eye perceives them most clearly.

GARDEN FEATURES

Ⓐ A teak dining table with light metal chairs forms the centrepiece.

Ⓑ The paved floor recedes visually into the background.

Ⓒ Evergreen mock privet acts as a canopy-forming shrub, providing cover and shade.

Ⓓ Pittosporum offers glossy foliage and year-round structure at mid-height.

Ⓔ Bamboo provides architectural foliage and movement with a dense, fan-like presence.

Ⓕ Fig adds Mediterranean character and textural contrast with its large, lobed leaves.

Ⓖ Climbing roses wind through the layered planting, adding vertical interest and early summer scent when they bloom.

Ⓗ Ginger lily (*Hedychium densiflorum* 'Stephen') brings a tropical note with bold foliage and late-summer flowers.

Ⓘ *Salvia* 'Amistad' has deep-violet blooms that contrast with green foliage.

Ⓙ African lily (*Agapanthus*) lines the edge with strappy leaves and clusters of sky-blue flowers.

5.

Perennial meadow
True meadows are a challenge to create and maintain. This one is just as attractive and much easier to plant.

Creating the impression of a true wildflower meadow is by no means an easy task, as traditional meadows require specific soil conditions and careful management to maintain a balanced mix of native grasses, flowers and shrubs. A perennial meadow offers a similarly rich and dynamic planting scheme and is far easier to establish and maintain.

This garden combines considered design with a sense of natural spontaneity, where tall grasses and flowering perennials weave together to create a tapestry of colour, texture and movement that changes with the seasons. Upkeep is easy: just cut back the dry stems and leaves by the end of the winter to make space for the new growth of the following season.

A neatly maintained path cuts through the planting, defining the space while allowing a close experience of the surrounding flora. The meadow is framed by perennial borders and an evergreen hedge at the back, adding depth and structure. Coneflowers, claries and scabious stand among ornamental grasses, their bold colours punctuating the soft, swaying grasses, while hydrangea 'Annabelle' provides a contrasting backdrop of voluminous, delicate blooms.

GARDEN FEATURES

Ⓐ Long grasses are cut back only once a year to maintain biodiversity.

Ⓑ A neatly defined lawn path ensures structure within the wilder planting.

Ⓒ Perennial borders enhance seasonal interest, complementing the looser planting.

Ⓓ An evergreen hedge provides year-round enclosure.

Ⓔ *Hydrangea arborescens* 'Annabelle' introduces a voluminous texture that contrasts with the meadow's natural feel.

Ⓕ Perennials with upright inflorescences, such as Balkan clary mimic the vertical movement of grasses.

Ⓖ Hardy perennials such as the daisy-like coneflowers bring striking colour and contrast into the scheme.

Ⓗ Scabious adds delicate, pollinator-friendly dome-shaped blooms, softening the transition between grasses and flowers.

Ⓘ Grasses, such as the fluffy hare's tail grass, are essential in creating the meadow's characteristic texture and movement. Also, many caterpillars feed on grasses, so if you want butterflies in your garden, you have to feed the larvae as well.

How to plant a perennial meadow

Above Scabious (*Scabiosa*).

Resilient and hardy plants

A successful perennial meadow needs deep-rooted, resilient plants that come back year after year. Perennials like fiery red and pink coneflowers (*Echinacea* spp.), Balkan clary (*Salvia nemorosa*) and scabious (*Scabiosa)* provide structure and colour, while self-seeding species like purple top (*Verbena bonariensis*) create a dynamic display. By choosing a diverse mix, you can ensure year-round interest, from early spring growth to seed heads that last into winter.

Ornamental grasses

Grasses create a natural framework for flowering perennials, adding texture and movement. Unlike traditional wildflower meadows, which can be tricky to get going, a perennial meadow benefits from ornamental grasses that provide structure all year round. Varieties such as hare's tail grass (*Lagurus ovatus*), muhly grass (*Muhlenbergia rigida*) and purple moor grass (*Molinia caerulea*) introduce soft, swaying textures that respond to wind and light.

Easy maintenance

Perennial meadows need far less maintenance than traditional lawns or wildflower meadows. You only need to cut them back once a year in late winter, which gives the plants time to self-seed. Avoid fertilizing and keep the soil conditions simple to help control overly vigorous growth and encourage a diverse mix of species. Regularly remove aggressive weeds.

Boundaries

Clear boundaries keep the planting looking intentional rather than unkempt. You could use a neatly mown lawn path, or use gravel edging to separate the meadow from other areas of the garden.

Embrace seasonal change

One of the best things about a perennial meadow is how it changes with the seasons. Spring brings fresh green shoots, while summer bursts into colour. In autumn, seed heads develop, adding texture and providing food for birds and other wildlife. Leaving these standing through winter keeps the garden looking interesting and supports biodiversity.

6.

Meditation garden
This garden is a living retreat, encouraging mindfulness and connection to nature.

Drawing inspiration from the layered landscapes of Chinese and Japanese garden traditions, this peaceful hideaway allows natural elements to take centre stage. It mixes organic materials, soft lighting and carefully chosen features to create a secluded space for calm reflection.

Sculptural tall shrubs like this wrinkled viburnum with lifted branches provide shelter and privacy from above while still keeping the space open. They also offer dappled shade, making soothing patterns of light on the garden floor. Beneath these, lush but restrained plantings of large-leaved shrubs like oak-leaved hydrangea and Japanese maples, ferns and a few ornamental perennials like foxgloves together create a rich tapestry of textures.

Evergreens, potted plants and verdant foliage provide balance, their considered placement echoing the refined simplicity of Zen aesthetics. The layout is fairly asymmetrical, mimicking natural landscapes rather than more formal arrangements.

A thoughtfully placed bell sculpture hangs down from a branch, where it might gently chime as birds alight, its soft tone enhancing the meditative atmosphere. It is a focal point that blends with nature and promotes visual harmony. The aim in this garden is not simply decoration but balance, simplicity and a deep connection to the natural world.

Above Japanese aralia (*Fatsia japonica*).

Above Hakone grass (*Hakonechloa macra*).

Plants for Asian-inspired gardens

NAME	HEIGHT	SPECIAL FEATURES
Japanese maple (*Acer palmatum*)	2–6m (6½–19½ft)	Elegant, deeply lobed leaves; fiery autumn colours; delicate branching.
Japanese aralia (*Fatsia japonica*)	1.5–3m (5–10ft)	Large, glossy evergreen leaves; tropical appearance; thrives in shade.
Hakone grass (*Hakonechloa macra*)	30–60cm (12–24in)	Soft, flowing foliage; adds movement and texture; ideal for shaded borders.
Plantain lily (*Hosta*)	30–80cm (12–31½in)	Lush, bold foliage; wide variety of textures and colours; thrives in shade.
Bamboo (*Phyllostachys*)	3–6m (10–19½ft)	Graceful, upright canes; striking dark stems; strong architectural presence.

GARDEN FEATURES

Ⓐ A bell sculpture introduces a soft, meditative soundscape, enhancing the garden's sense of tranquillity.

Ⓑ A small wooden seating area with flexible folding chairs invites stillness.

Ⓒ Tall shrubs with lifted branches create a serene canopy, allowing filtered light to reach the plants below.

Ⓓ Shrubs such as oak-leaved hydrangea (*Hydrangea quercifolia*), its deeply lobed leaves offering interesting seasonal colour, contribute to the garden's textural appeal.

Ⓔ Evergreen plantings provide year-round structure and are the backbone of the garden, offering a sense of permanence amid the changing seasons. Here laurustinus (*Viburnum tinus*), camellias and the climbing Henry's honeysuckle (*Lonicera henryi*) form a dense, jungle-like planting.

Ⓕ Small potted plants like these foxgloves add detail and variation, making use of different heights and textures.

Ⓖ Large-leaved evergreens like wrinkled viburnum (*Viburnum rhytidophyllum*) and rhododendron provide depth and create an intimate atmosphere.

7.

Hillside rockery

Sculptural rocks, a steep incline and wild grasses create a naturalistic garden on a challenging plot.

Transforming a steep slope into a functional and visually striking garden requires a balance of natural materials, structured planting and smart design solutions. This garden design embraces the site's elevation, working with rather than against the natural terrain.

Strategically placed boulders and stepping stones create stability, preventing erosion and providing planting pockets while enhancing the sculptural aesthetic. The artful placement and varying sizes of the rocks makes it appear as though they've always been there, and low-maintenance, drought-tolerant plants thrive in between them. Tall ornamental grasses like purple moor-grass near the stairs and Chinese silver grass soften the hard edges of the stone, adding movement and contrast to the solid structures.

Gravel surfaces and wooden decking make it easy to move around, keeping the space practical but still in harmony with its surroundings. A focal point of the garden is a fire bowl, offering warmth and a space to congregate, while a reflective water feature integrated into stone introduces a dynamic element, mirroring the sky and surrounding greenery. The result is a garden that celebrates its position, blending rugged textures with refined design.

Considerations for hillside gardens

Erosion control

Sloping gardens are prone to erosion and water run-off, so structural reinforcement is essential. Large boulders or stacked stone walls provide stability and prevent soil movement. Terracing also improves water retention, reducing the risk of run-off and erosion.

Structure

Breaking up a steep slope into tiered levels maximizes the usability of the space. Each level can serve a different function, such as a seating area or planting zone. Plan for safe and easy access with stepping stones, gravel paths or stone stairs. This makes planting and upkeep manageable without disturbing the structure or compacting the soil too much.

Plant selection

Traditional lawns can be difficult to maintain on a slope. Instead choose drought-tolerant, sun-loving and slope-hardy plants like prairie perennials or ornamental grasses. Opt for low-maintenance species that thrive in rocky, well-drained soil and offer seasonal interest.

Focal points

A well-placed fire pit, water feature or sculptural element adds purpose and interest. These focal points not only draw the eye through the space, but also provide functional gathering areas. A reflective water basin built into a rock enhances the sensory experience.

Above Japanese holly (*Ilex crenata*).

Above Chinese silver grass (*Miscanthus sinensis*).

GARDEN FEATURES

Ⓐ Wooden steps and decking with smooth surfaces provide safe access, reducing the risk of slipping compared to ridged steps.

Ⓑ Large natural rocks are strategically placed to stabilize the slope and contribute to the rugged aesthetic.

Ⓒ Stone steps in a complementary shade integrate with the natural rock elements.

Ⓓ A fire bowl creates a central focal point.

Ⓔ Gravel offers a practical, low-maintenance surface that aids in drainage and erosion control.

Ⓕ Tall ornamental grasses like purple moor grass (*Molinia caerulea* subsp. *arundinacea* 'Skyracer') add a soft, wild contrast to the hard stone, introducing movement and seasonal interest.

Ⓖ A small retaining wall defines the space and serves as a seating area.

Ⓗ A sculptural stone water feature provides a reflective surface that mirrors the sky, attracting wildlife and adding a tranquil atmosphere.

Ⓘ Chinese silver grass (*Miscanthus sinensis* 'Adagio') has grey-green leaves that turn orange and yellow in autumn.

Ⓙ Japanese holly (*Ilex crenata* 'Convexa') thrives best in well-drained soil, in full sun to partial shade.

8.

Hydrangea heaven
Small gardens don't have to mean small plantings. This fragrant shrub anchors the space and offers seasonal drama.

At this garden's heart, the showy hydrangea 'Annabelle' provides a striking focal point. Its clusters of glowing white flowers brighten the space and contrast against the deep green cherry laurel hedging. The large, rounded flower heads start off green, maturing to a snowy white in summer, before fading back to soft green in early autumn.

A series of neutral grey stepping stones weaves through a dense carpet of mind-your-own-business, a delicate, low-maintenance ground cover that is prized for its lush, moss-like appearance, which spills out of the gaps and enhances the natural flow of the space. The path leads to a defined seating area, where darker timber flooring sets it apart. The furniture is lightweight and elegant in a subdued palette, carefully chosen to blend into the surroundings rather than compete with the centrepiece flowering shrub.

Common ivy climbs the walls, which softens the hard edges and provides greenery all year round. The mix of materials and plants makes the garden feel compact and peaceful, showing that a well-planned space can be both practical and visually pleasing.

GARDEN FEATURES

Ⓐ Stepping stones in neutral grey are softened by the surrounding ground cover.

Ⓑ Mind-your-own-business (*Soleirolia soleirolii*) is a living carpet that fills the gaps between stepping stones, creating a green underlayer that requires little maintenance.

Ⓒ A seating area with timber flooring provides a warm contrast to the stone pathway.

Ⓓ Lightweight, elegant furniture maintains a refined aesthetic, ensuring the seating blends into the design.

Ⓔ *Hydrangea arborescens* 'Annabelle' as a focal point creates seasonal interest with large, white flowers that bloom through the whole summer. The shrub can grow up to 1–1.5m (3–5ft) both tall and wide.

Ⓕ Cherry laurel (*Prunus laurocerasus*) as a privacy hedge forms a dense green backdrop, defining the garden's boundaries.

Ⓖ Common ivy (*Hedera helix*) provides vertical coverage, softening hard surfaces and adding an evergreen layer.

Ⓗ A solitary fern and a masterwort (*Astrantia*) frame the path to the sitting area.

Types of hydrangea

Above *Hydrangea paniculata*.

Bigleaf

Known for its rounded flower heads, *Hydrangea macrophylla* offers bold summer colour in shades of blue, pink or mauve depending on soil pH (blue in acidic soil, pink in neutral or alkaline soil). Its full, leafy presence is ideal for adding drama to borders. Best grown in moist, well-drained soil with afternoon shade. 'Runaway Bride' is loved for its cascading habit and profuse flowering. Unlike typical hydrangeas, it produces blooms not only at the tips but all along the arching stems.

Saw-toothed

A more delicate cousin of the bigleaf, *Hydrangea serrata* features flatter, lacecap blooms surrounded by tiny, fertile flowers. Native to the mountains of Japan, it's exceptionally hardy and perfect for more naturalistic or woodland-style gardens. Foliage often turns brilliant red or burgundy in autumn.

Smooth

Valued for its resilience, *Hydrangea arborescens* produces large, domed heads of creamy white blooms from early to late summer. Varieties like the white 'Annabelle' and 'Pink Annabelle' are especially prized for their enormous flower heads. Thriving in partial shade, it can also tolerate more sun with adequate moisture, and is less fussy about soil conditions.

Oakleaf

Distinct for its handsome, lobed foliage that resembles oak leaves, *Hydrangea quercifolia* brings multi-season interest: conical clusters of creamy flowers in summer, burgundy foliage in autumn and handsome bark in winter. It thrives in well-drained soil and partial shade.

Panicled

The adaptable *Hydrangea paniculata* bears large, upright cones of flowers that shift from white to pink as they age. It's an excellent choice for sunny or lightly shaded sites. 'Limelight' and 'Vanille Fraise' are popular cultivars known for spectacular colour changes.

Sargent

Hydrangea aspera subsp. *sargentiana* is prized for its large, velvety leaves and broad, flat lacecap flowers in lilac to deep mauve shades. The textured foliage adds a tactile dimension to shady borders. Flowering from mid to late summer, it brings colour to darker garden areas. Best grown in fertile soil with consistent moisture and light to medium shade. It is well suited to woodland gardens.

Climbing

An exceptional climber, *Hydrangea petiolaris* var. *anomala* anchors itself to walls and trees with aerial roots. It produces elegant sprays of creamy white, lightly fragrant lacecap flowers in early summer. Thriving in shade or semi-shade, it's perfect for covering north-facing walls and bringing vertical structure.

9.

Gravel garden

An eco-friendly design, ideal for showcasing drought-tolerant plants in a natural setting with minimal upkeep.

Gravel gardens have long been favoured by designers seeking resilient beauty. Inspired by pioneers such as Beth Chatto – whose famous dry garden in Essex, UK, demonstrated her philosophy of 'right plant, right place' – they have been adapted by landscape designer Dan Pearson for the new Delos garden in Sissinghurst, Kent and renowned plantsman Peter Janke at Hortvs for his garden in Hilden, Germany.

This planting style celebrates the potential of harsh, free-draining conditions. With minimal irrigation, no traditional lawn and a naturalistic palette of drought-tolerant plants, gravel gardens offer a sustainable response to changing climate and lifestyle needs.

This garden applies these principles at a smaller scale. Stepping stones provide access through a layered composition of grasses and late-summer perennials. The gravel functions as both mulch and a design element, controlling weeds, improving drainage and setting a neutral tone for the planting.

Structural grasses including feather reed grass, Chinese silver grass and golden oats form the backbone of the scheme, their upright forms adding rhythm and movement. Interwoven with them, purple top and fine-leaved Mexican feather grass provide rich texture, colour and biodiversity.

Benefits of gravel gardens

Less water required

Gravel gardens are designed around plants that thrive in dry conditions. Once established, they require little to no supplementary watering, making them ideal in regions facing hotter summer temperatures or restrictions on water use.

Greater diversity

Freed from the monoculture of turf, gravel gardens can host a dynamic mix of grasses, self-seeding perennials and drought-adapted species. This encourages a greater range of pollinators, insects and soil organisms, enhancing the ecological value of your garden.

Fewer weeds

Gravel mulch acts as a natural barrier, suppressing weed growth by limiting light and making germination more difficult. This reduces the need for regular weeding.

Healthier soil

Without the compaction caused by frequent maintenance, and thanks to excellent drainage, the soil beneath a gravel garden supports strong root development and healthy microbial life. Also, the layer of gravel, which should be approximately 10cm (4in) thick, prevents evaporation and keeps the soil moist and cool.

Lower maintenance

There is no need for continual mowing, edging or irrigation. Gravel gardens are shaped by seasonal change, not constant intervention. Occasional editing and replanting are all that is needed to maintain their character and structure.

Remove the stems and leaves of perennials and grasses in late winter or cut them back, depending on the type of planting. It's important to tidy plantings inspired by the steppe and Mediterranean shrubland, which are full of plants that can grow in dry, nutrient-poor soil, as extra organic matter encourages too much growth.

Right Purple top (*Verbena bonariensis*).

GARDEN FEATURES

Ⓐ Stepping stones playfully break up the space and facilitate access, minimizing disturbance to the plantings.

Ⓑ Gravel mulch prevents weeds and reduces the need for irrigation.

Ⓒ Chinese silver grass (*Miscanthus sinensis* 'Gracillimus') adds height and texture with arching foliage that moves gracefully in the wind.

Ⓓ Golden oats grass (*Stipa gigantea*) features tall, airy verticals with radiant flowers that shimmer in the sun and persist into winter.

Ⓔ Feather reed grass (*Calamagrostis* × *acutiflora* 'Karl Foerster') provides vertical structure with a compact, upright habit that remains well into the colder months.

Ⓕ Mexican feather grass (*Stipa tenuissima*) softens edges with fine, downy foliage that sways with the lightest breeze.

Ⓖ Purple top (*Verbena bonariensis*) provides colour, weaving through the grasses.

Ⓗ Mexican fleabane (*Erigeron karvinskianus*) spreads over the gravel.

Ⓘ Small perennials like thrift (*Armeria maritima*) fill the narrow spaces between stepping stones.

10.

Sponge garden
A stylish, sustainable design that turns every downpour into a win for both your garden and the planet.

With climate change bringing increasingly frequent extreme weather events, including sudden downpours and prolonged dry spells, the way we design our gardens must evolve. This sponge garden embraces the challenge by working with water, not against it, prioritizing permeability, plant cover and low-impact materials. It draws on the principles of sustainable urban drainage, where hard surfaces are minimized and rainfall is slowed, absorbed and filtered naturally through soil and planting.

This small garden demonstrates how these principles can be applied. A simple gravel and stone path replaces a conventional lawn, trickling rainwater gently through the space. Beds are densely planted with moisture-absorbing perennials, shrubs and ground covers, while large-leaved species like umbrella plants help to capture and slow rainfall. Planting the boundaries and using evergreen screens offers privacy and shelter, while also helping to shield against the wind and regulate the microclimate to create a cool and pleasant atmosphere, even during the hot summer months.

Instead of a sealed patio, a modest sitting area is integrated into the garden floor with loose slabs surrounded by gravel, which allows water to pass through easily. The result is a garden that feels intimate, flourishing and quietly resilient.

GARDEN FEATURES

- (A) Stone slabs are laid directly onto a permeable substrate, allowing rain to drain between joints.
- (B) Mixed paving integrates gravel and irregular stones to support natural drainage along the path.
- (C) Umbrella plant (*Darmera peltata*) helps catch rainwater with its large, textured leaves, sending it directly to the root system.
- (D) A small seating area of weathered stone slabs and upcycled furniture minimizes overuse of hard surfacing.
- (E) Planted boundaries combine shrubs, climbers and tall perennials for wind protection, privacy and rain interception.
- (F) Gravel extensions create flexibility, ideal for placing extra chairs without sealing over more soil.
- (G) Dense planting ensures year-round soil cover, reduces erosion and maximizes rain absorption.
- (H) Witch hazel (*Hamamelis*) is famous for its bright, fragrant flowers and stunning autumn colour.
- (I) Hemp agrimony (*Eupatorium cannabium*) reaches a height of up to 1.5–2m (5–6½ft) and is a haven for pollinators.
- (J) Meadow rue (*Thalictrum*), another tall perennial that thrives in moist conditions.

Build a weather-resilient garden

Open surfaces
Prioritize surfaces that let water in. Gravel paths, loose-laid pavers, bark mulch and permeable jointing between paving stones allow rainfall to soak into the ground, replenishing soil moisture and reducing run-off.

Reduce paving
Limit non-permeable areas and avoid concrete and tightly grouted surfaces. By scaling down seating zones and walkways, you make more room for planting and reduce the risk of flash flooding during or after heavy downpours.

Small is beautiful
A compact seating area meets everyday needs while reducing the amount of hard surfacing. Temporary extensions, such as gravel patches for extra chairs, offer flexibility without sealing the soil.

Plants as infrastructure
Dense planting with overlapping canopies intercepts rainfall, shades the soil and reduces evaporation. Roots create micro-channels that help water be absorbed into the ground and improve soil structure over time.

Use moisture-loving species
In areas where water collects, include plants such as Siberian iris (*Iris sibirica*), meadowsweet (*Filipendula ulmaria*) or umbrella plant to help manage moisture naturally.

Above Meadowsweet (*Filipendula ulmaria*).

Tall boundary planting
Shrubs and tall perennials at the garden's edge create shelter from wind, trap humidity and provide privacy. These living barriers also reduce the drying effects of wind, helping the garden hold on to moisture.

Store water on-site
Integrate rainwater harvesting with water butts or underground tanks. Let gravel or rain gardens act as temporary reservoirs, allowing excess rain to drain slowly through planted beds.

11.

Pocket patio

With natural materials, textured planting and vertical elements, the smallest spaces can have a big impact.

The most bijou outdoor space can be reimagined as a richly planted retreat. This compact courtyard shows how a few square metres, when carefully designed, can offer a lush, seasonal and highly personal garden experience. Without the need for a lawn or extensive hard landscaping, the space is filled with texture and colour, an oasis of calm enveloped in greenery.

At its heart is a narrow path of natural stone slabs, flanked by densely planted borders and leading to a slim bistro-style table and chairs. Every element has been deliberately selected for maximum flexibility and visual impact.

Foliage plays a starring role, with architectural plants like angel wings and fennel creating highlights and contrast. Flowering perennials and self-seeding annuals are woven between them for colour and movement, while upright plants like ornamental ginger and salvias add height and enclosure. In such a small footprint, each plant has to earn its place, bringing either long-season interest or strong structural value. The result is a vibrant garden that invites you into its relaxing embrace.

Design ideas for tiny courtyards

Forgo the lawn

In very small gardens, lawns consume precious space without offering proportionate visual or ecological benefit. Replacing turf with natural stone, gravel or densely planted borders opens up the design. These reduce maintenance needs and allow for layered planting that brings interest across seasons.

Versatile furniture

Furniture should be comfortable, lightweight and easy to stow. Foldable metal chairs and bistro tables, as used here, strike a balance between elegance and flexibility. They can be rearranged for a solitary coffee or removed entirely when repotting plants. Choosing grey or dark finishes also helps integrate them into the planting.

Dense planting

In a small space, layering adds drama and depth. Rather than leaving open ground, filling beds with a mix of small shrubs, ground covers and perennials creates a feeling of abundance. Dense planting shades the soil, helping to retain moisture and reduce weed growth, so minimizing upkeep. Select species with overlapping growth habits and staggered bloom times to enjoy year-round colour, texture and structure.

Above Angel wings (*Senecio candidans* 'Angel Wings').

Evergreens for structure

Tiny gardens will benefit from a few permanent features that hold the design together through the seasons. Compact evergreen shrubs like yew (*Taxus baccata*) and bay (*Laurus nobilis*), or architectural perennials such as angel wings (*Senecio candidans* 'Angel Wings') act as visual anchors. Planted at corners, around seats or along paths, they bring structure, contrast and winter interest to an otherwise changing display.

Perennials and annuals for variety

Perennials provide dependable, long-season structure, while annuals inject spontaneity and brightness. Combining the two allows for both continuity and change. In small spaces, this constant evolution keeps the experience fresh.

GARDEN FEATURES

Ⓐ Natural stone slabs form a narrow path that divides the planting beds and gives access to the seating area without dominating the design.

Ⓑ Foldable seating ensures functionality and flexibility in a tight space.

Ⓒ Roseleaf sage (*Salvia involucrata* 'Bethellii') adds height, scent and colour late into the season.

Ⓓ Tall purple top (*Verbena bonariensis*) introduces airy structure and is beloved by butterflies.

Ⓔ Angel wings create dramatic silver contrast.

Ⓕ Begonias offer long-lasting colour and bold foliage.

Ⓖ Fennel (*Foeniculum vulgare*) lends movement and fine texture while supporting pollinators.

Ⓗ Roses contribute structure and colour.

Ⓘ Ginger lily (*Hedychium* spp.) provides lush foliage and late-summer blooms.

Ⓙ Cape daisies (*Osteospermum* spp.) flower prolifically in sunny positions.

12.

Biodiverse borders
Create a vibrant, peaceful sanctuary that nurtures local ecosystems.

The garden's design embraces elements that will attract and support an array of wildlife. Perennial borders invite bees, butterflies and other insects to feed. Tall grasses add texture and movement, while native plants provide dense ground cover and a habitat for nesting birds and small mammals.

A meandering cobbled path leads through lush vegetation and invites visitors to immerse themselves in the garden's natural diversity. A dry stone wall separates it from the even wilder area behind. Wall-nesting solitary bees, spiders, beetles and the occasional lizard enjoy the warmth of the stones as well as the shelter they provide.

The door is made of reclaimed wood and hung between brick columns. The solid oak is long lasting and provides a foraging opportunity for wasps to collect wood fibres for their nests and a nesting space for tree-boring bees.

Roses and aquilegias add splashes of colour, their blooms serving as a pollen and nectar source for insects. These vibrant accents punctuate the greenery, infusing the garden with an enchanting sense of vitality and life. In this naturalistic haven, every element tells a story of beauty found in imperfection, and of the bond between us and the natural world.

How to create a supportive eco garden

Native plants
Incorporate a diverse selection of native plants, including perennials, grasses, shrubs and trees that thrive in your local climate and soil conditions. Native plants are a source of food and shelter for wildlife and require less maintenance.

Irregular planting
Embrace irregular planting patterns to mimic the randomness of nature. Opt for a more organic layout, allowing plants to grow freely and intermingle with one another for an untamed look.

Natural materials
Use natural materials such as stone, wood and gravel to create paths, borders and structures within the garden. Incorporate elements like cobbled paths, wooden benches and dead wood to create microhabitats for a wide variety of wildlife.

Wildlife habitat
Design the garden to provide habitat and food sources for all wildlife, including birds, mammals, reptiles and amphibians, as well as the many insects like butterflies and wild bees. Incorporate bird feeders, nesting boxes and nesting aids for insects, fostering a thriving ecosystem within the garden.

Seasonal interest
Ensure year-round interest as well as a consistent source of food and shelter for wildlife by selecting plants that offer seasonal blooms, foliage colour and textural variation. Incorporate a mix of early spring bulbs, summer-flowering perennials and autumn grasses to create an ever-changing landscape that delights the senses throughout the year. For additional autumn interest, add prairie perennials like coneflowers (*Echinacea* and *Rudbeckia*), asters or salvias. These provide nectar and pollen when other flora have reached their peak.

Left Yellow archangel (*Lamium galeobdolon*).

GARDEN FEATURES

Ⓐ A cobbled stone path creates a winding route through the garden and blends into the planting.

Ⓑ The reclaimed wooden door gives a sense of enclosure, while its rough texture and warm tones integrate with the surroundings.

Ⓒ A red brick wall provides a characterful backdrop.

Ⓓ A wooden bench made from salvaged timber offers a place to sit, and provides nooks and crannies for insects.

Ⓔ Native shrubs such as dogwood (*Cornus sanguinea*) and hawthorn (*Crataegus monogyna*) provide structure, food and shelter for birds and insects year-round.

Ⓕ Red campion (*Silene vulgaris*) adds seasonal interest with bright colours, long flowering periods and strong wildlife appeal.

Ⓖ Groundcover planting with species like wild violets (*Viola*) and yellow archangel (*Lamium galeobdolon*) helps suppress weeds, retain moisture and support a healthy soil ecosystem.

13.

Equatorial retreat
Evoke tropical climes with palms, ferns and succulents for a serene, exotic atmosphere.

Even if your garden is far from the equator, it's still possible to cultivate the look and feel of the tropics. This narrow garden proves how a carefully curated collection of exotic plants, housed in containers and gravel beds, can recreate the atmosphere of a desert garden or a coastal resort. By combining structure, texture and a little seasonal movement, this design leads the eye along a central path, showcasing bold, layered planting on either side.

In this garden, its setting has an additional advantage, as two different microclimates have been created. On the dry and sunnier left side, yucca and agave thrive in containers and pots, and Mediterranean perennials and semi-shrubs like wormwood fill the cracks between the stones. The right side (see page 140), which sits in partial shade, supports more moisture-tolerant plants such as barrenwort and hardy banana.

Despite the exotic palette, this garden remains manageable with good drainage and regular checks when watering and fertilizing. The main obstacle to avoid is buying too many new plants during the summer and not having enough space for overwintering them.

GARDEN FEATURES

Ⓐ Mexican grass tree (*Nolina longifolia*) provides strong vertical form with its strappy leaves.

Ⓑ A small stone gate palm (*Trachycarpus princeps*) adds a rounded, textural silhouette.

Ⓒ Potted yucca delivers bold structure in containers.

Ⓓ Hardy banana (*Musa basjoo*) offers large, tropical foliage and an exotic focal point.

Ⓔ The *Yucca queretaroensis* planted directly into the soil needs excellent drainage.

Ⓕ Sago palms (*Cycas revoluta*) are housed in pots or sheltered niches. They need protection from frost.

Ⓖ Sunny-side planting includes drought-tolerant species such as wormwood (*Artemisia*).

Ⓗ Barrenwort (*Epimedium × perralchicum*) grows in the cooler, shaded areas, offering ground cover and contrasting softness.

Ⓘ A sculptural focal point placed at the end of the path draws the eye through the garden.

Create an exotic container garden

Drainage is key

Exotic plants – especially succulents, palms and desert-adapted species – dislike wet feet. Ensure containers have large drainage holes, and always place a layer of grit or coarse stone at the base of the pot. Raised beds and gravel surfaces support faster drying and oxygen exchange around the roots.

Use mineral substrates

Choose lean, fast-draining soil mixes rich in sand, perlite, pumice or crushed lava. Avoid compost-rich soil that retains too much moisture: these plants thrive in tough, mineral-based media.

Acclimatize plants gradually

After winter protection indoors or in a greenhouse, harden plants slowly in spring. Sudden exposure to sun, wind or cool night temperatures can cause stress or leaf scorch in tender species.

Regular seasonal checks

Inspect pots frequently for pests, rot or signs of waterlogging like floppy leaves, especially after heavy rain. Lift or rotate pots as needed to balance light and temperature across them.

Think like a traveller

Design your space with a holiday mood in mind. Group plants that remind you of specific landscapes: Mediterranean terraces, Mexican deserts, Balinese courtyards. The associations are all part of the experience.

Top Hardy banana (*Musa basjoo*).
Bottom Bitter wormwood (*Artemesia absinthium*).

Structured design brings order to outdoor spaces. Even in naturalistic settings, carefully placed elements can anchor a garden, help guide movement and create a balance of softness and precision.

STRUCTURED GARDENS

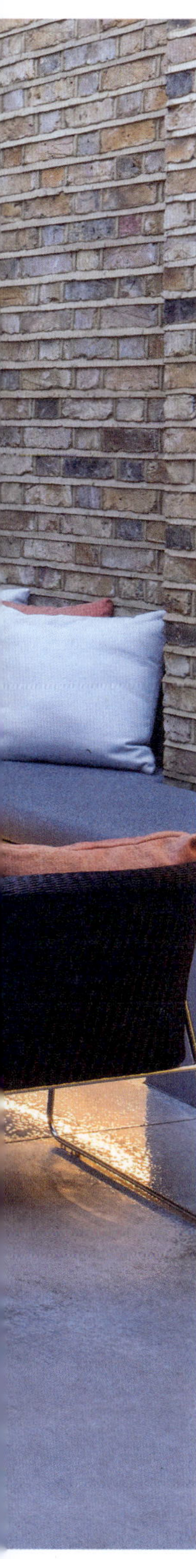

1.

Walled garden

This multilevel enclosed garden creates a sense of intimacy, its microclimate protecting delicate plants.

This sunken terrace within a walled garden combines architectural precision with layered planting. The clean lines of the flat stone terrace reinforce the contemporary aesthetic, and a built-in bench with integrated lighting enhances the ambiance. The space is defined by a tiered concrete retaining wall, which not only supports the upper level but also serves as an elevated planting bed.

Trimmed boxwood at the lower level and clipped bamboo above, illuminated from below, introduce structure and texture. To soften the strong lines, African lily fills the mid-layers and carefully spaced hakone grass adds seasonal interest on the top terrace. The cool, dark green foliage is punctuated by occasional architectural accents – such as the globe flowers of the African lily – that echo the garden's graphic geometry.

A small tree with a shaped trunk provides a sculptural focal point for the upper dining terrace, offering shade and a contrast to the surrounding darker greenery. To further soften the architectural elements, evergreen ivy cascades along the walls, interspersed with dark purple flowering clematis, enveloping the garden and providing privacy and a much-needed wildlife habitat.

How to plant a walled garden

Embrace shade

Walled gardens often create cool, shaded microclimates. Take advantage of this by selecting shade-tolerant plants such as ferns, hostas and hydrangeas. Introduce dappled light with trellised climbers like clematis or wisteria, integrated lighting or reflective surfaces to brighten darker corners.

Create different levels

Tiered planting beds, raised terraces and sunken seating areas add depth and dimension. Vertical layers help maximize space.

Think of the garden as room

A walled garden should feel like an extension of the home. Define functional areas with seating, pathways and focal points such as a fireplace, water feature or sculptural tree. Consider outdoor furniture and decorative elements that echo interior styling.

Mix formal with informal elements

Balance structured hardscaping with naturalistic planting. Use geometric pathways or clipped hedging to contrast with looser, more organic planting arrangements, softening the rigid lines.

Seasonal Interest

Ensure year-round appeal by combining early spring bulbs like crocus, daffodils or tulips, summer-flowering perennials like salvias, spurges (*Euphorbia*) or ornamental alliums, and grasses for an impact in autumn.

Above *Clematis* 'Polish Spirit'.

Green walls

Vertical planting not only saves precious ground space but also softens hard surfaces and improves air quality. Plant climbers at the base of the wall or fence, either self-attaching species like common ivy (*Hedera helix*), trumpet vine (*Campsis*) or Boston ivy (*Parthenocissus*), or winding species like wisteria, honeysuckle (*Lonicera*) or chocolate vine (*Akebia quinata*).

Stylish but requiring a lot of maintenance are green walls where perennials, grasses and small shrubs are grown in small pockets. These green wall systems should have a built-in irrigation system, be positioned to receive filtered light, and protected from heat, sun and strong winds.

GARDEN FEATURES

- (A) A stone terrace grounds the overall composition.
- (B) A built-in bench with integrated lighting combines comfort with atmospheric illumination.
- (C) Lightweight furniture ensues versatility.
- (D) A structured concrete retaining wall supports the upper level and functions as a raised planting bed.
- (E) Trimmed evergreen boxwood (*Buxus sempervirens*) introduces a formal element.
- (F) Clipped bamboo (*Phyllostachys*) creates a striking effect with its illuminated foliage.
- (G) An elevated dining terrace provides an additional seating area.
- (H) A sculpted small tree provides shade and serves as a focal point.
- (I) Evergreen ivy enhances the sense of enclosure. Dark purple clematis (*Clematis* 'Polish Spirit') brings colour to the otherwise dark background.
- (J) African lily (*Agapanthus* 'Black Pantha') introduces seasonal colour and height.
- (K) Hakone grass (*Hakonechloa macra*) sways over the edge of the container.

2.

Structured courtyard
An ordered Zen space that requires minimum maintenance.

This geometrically pleasing courtyard garden blends structured hardscaping with formal plantings to create a Zen-like retreat. Large Yorkstone slabs are interspersed with polished blue pebbles and a reddish toned gravel, forming a striking graphic pattern that underlines the space's architectural quality. A concrete fireplace serves as a focal point, anchoring the outdoor seating area, which incorporates durable weatherproof furniture.

The planting palette introduces layers of texture and movement, offsetting the more orderly, fixed elements. Clump-forming grasses are intentionally planted in the gravel beds, their feathery forms contrasting with the mirrored garden orbs, which reflect the changing light and add sculptural interest.

Multistemmed magnolias provide height and seasonal beauty, while a wooden fence in muted blue-grey tones echoes the pebbles, creating a cohesive effect. Soft and stiffer grasses add further depth, alongside bronze-leaved shrubs and a Japanese maple, whose delicate green foliage introduces a fresh element.

GARDEN FEATURES

(A) Yorkstone slabs create a structured foundation.

(B) Pebbles enhance permeability and provide textural contrast.

(C) A concrete fireplace acts as a sculptural centrepiece.

(D) Furniture is aligned with the linear pattern.

(E) Feathery grasses on the gravel bed softens the hardscaping.

(F) Different-sized orbs are grouped for a bold feature, giving the feel of a sculpture garden.

(G) Multistemmed magnolia add structure and year-round shade. Fairly pest-resistant, they are easy to maintain once established.

(H) Soft Balkan blue grass (*Sesleria heufleriana*) introduces a gentle, flowing texture.

(I) Autumn moor-grass (*Sesleria autumnalis*) offers a more rigid, upright growth habit.

(J) Small shrubs with bronze-red foliage echo the gravel tone.

(K) The compact Japanese maple is ideal for small courtyards and has a sculptural appeal.

Creating a formal courtyard design

Limit materials for cohesion
Keep the palette of hard materials restrained: three is often the magic number. Here, Yorkstone slabs form the base, gravel is used between pavers to aid drainage and metallic spheres act as a sculptural punctuation. Repeating these tones and textures gives a calm, composed feel. Choose materials like natural stone and stainless steel, which age gracefully and require little upkeep.

Embrace repetition and geometry
Use repetition of shapes and colours to unify the space. In this garden, linear planting echoes the layout of the hardscape and the grey paving is picked up by the tones of the fence, grasses and sculptures. Furniture and a geometric fireplace align with the grid-like structure, reinforcing the formality. The grid also allows flexibility, where individual elements can be updated without disrupting the overall rhythm.

Grasses and evergreen structure
To maintain structure throughout the seasons with minimal effort, combine evergreens with textural grasses. Use clump-forming species for their neat, architectural form. Seslerias are tolerant of dry soils and require only a yearly trim. In shadier areas, compact Japanese maple (*Acer palmatum*) or small-leaved magnolias with rich foliage tones add form without fuss.

Add interest through accent planting
Rather than mixing in lots of varieties, group feathery grasses for soft movement and introduce seasonal bulbs like alliums or tulips for a spring highlight. The look remains ordered, but with just enough change to keep the space interesting. Fewer species mean less maintenance.

Keep planting minimal and easy-care
This garden is designed to look sharp with very little input. Grasses are long-lived and drought-tolerant, requiring only one tidy-up per year. Trees like multistemmed magnolias give height and volume without demanding constant pruning. Pebbled areas suppress weeds and the absence of a lawn means there's no mowing at all.

Right Autumn moor grass (*Sesleria autumnalis*).

3.

Sensory garden
Enjoy the calming embrace of nature in a serene space for contemplation and meditation.

This secluded garden has been carefully crafted to engage all five senses, encouraging stillness and awareness of the natural world. Nestled beneath a lush canopy, the design blends structure with informality. A simple layout of stepping stones and a dark pergola frames the space, while vertical planting and architectural trees add height and a feeling of enclosed intimacy.

Soft planting, including ferns, birches, willows and climbers, provides movement and texture, while elements such as wind chimes and a sculptural table introduce subtle sounds and tactile detail. The palette of greens is punctuated by seasonal highlights, from colourful spring tulips to the fine foliage of weeping willow. Wisteria, star jasmine and clematis introduce delicate perfume.

Light and shadow play through the pergola, shifting through the day to create a meditative atmosphere. Sensory richness comes from contrasts: soft against strong, light against dark and wild against ordered. This garden is a quiet, grounded counterpoint to daily life, where the interplay of whispering leaves, gentle chimes, soft scent and hypnotic movement transforms a compact space into a serene sanctuary.

How to create a sensory garden

Vertical elements

Structures such as pergolas, arches or trellised screens enclose the garden and offer privacy. They also support climbers such as wisteria, star jasmine (*Trachelospermum jasminoides*) and clematis, which introduce scent, shade and softness. Dappled light through overhead planting adds to the immersive quality.

Containers for flexibility

Pots allow you to bring focal points of scent and texture into close proximity. Choose tactile containers like glazed ceramic, weathered stone or rusted metal and fill them with aromatic herbs like lavender, lemon balm (*Melissa officinalis*) or scented pelargoniums. In shaded areas, pots of hostas or hakone grass (*Hakonechloa macra*) can soften hard edges with luxuriant foliage.

Sound for tranquillity

Introduce gentle soundscapes to mask urban noise. Wind chimes hung from a shaded pergola add soft, musical notes. A small water feature creates a consistent trickle that encourages contemplation. Rustling plants such as ornamental grasses can also enhance the auditory experience on breezy days.

Reduce and refine

Resist the temptation to overload the garden with variety. A limited palette of greens, whites and silvers brings calm, while layering leaf textures adds complexity. Consider how each material contributes to the atmosphere: gravel underfoot, smooth stone surfaces and weathered wood all add to the garden's sensory richness.

Sophisticated contrasts

Contrast is key to engaging the senses. Pair light and dark foliage, and upright forms with trailing silhouettes. Mix structural evergreens with seasonal highlights like ornamental bulbs to ensure that there is always something to notice. A combination of formality and wildness creates an evocative balance.

Right Weeping willow (*Salix babylonica*).

GARDEN FEATURES

Ⓐ A path of sandstone slabs is set in gravel.

Ⓑ The pergola provides overhead shade and a framework for climbers.

Ⓒ Wisteria provides scent and colour in spring, and Dutchman's pipe (*Aristolochia macrophylla*) brings broad architectural foliage.

Ⓓ Metallic wind chimes provide a soft melody with every breeze.

Ⓔ Silver birch (*Betula pendula*) offers a light-filtering canopy and delicate bark texture.

Ⓕ Soft shield ferns (*Polystichum setiferum*) and lady ferns (*Athyrium filix-femina*) provide feathery contrast and a lush, forest floor feel.

Ⓖ Soft shades of tulips near the secluded bench offer a short-lived but powerful burst of spring colour.

Ⓗ A weeping willow (*Salix babylonica*) adds both drama and delicacy, with long, trailing stems that catch the light.

Ⓘ Japanese maple (*Acer japonicum* 'Aconitifolium') delivers standout foliage colour in autumn in an otherwise green palette.

Ⓙ The stone table is a tactile focal point with an Ikebana-style planting placed on top.

4.

Split-level garden
Play around with height and balance hard and soft features to open up a small, multilevel space.

This once dark and closed-off lower ground floor space has been turned into a stylish terrace that leads onto a bright, greenery-filled garden. By using clean lines, smart planting and top-quality materials, the design makes the sunken terrace and the raised garden above appear as one continuous space.

The lower level features a formal arrangement of tall, slim planters that hold tidy boxwood balls. These create a striking sculptural feature while adding year-round greenery. An elegant stairway made from finestone leads up to the main garden, softening the transition between levels while complementing the warm tones of the surrounding wood panelling.

The upper level offers a more naturalistic space, featuring ornamental grasses, flowering perennials and a small lawn that introduces a softer, more relaxed atmosphere. A multistemmed serviceberry provides dappled shade, while evergreen climbers like star jasmine and a hedge of cherry laurel add texture and privacy. A seating area at the top of the garden includes weatherproof outdoor loungers, perfect for relaxing.

Above Star jasmine (*Trachelospermum jasminoides*).

Compact evergreen climbers

NAME	HEIGHT	SPECIAL FEATURES
Star jasmine (*Trachelospermum jasminoides*)	Up to 3m (10ft)	Fragrant white flowers, glossy green leaves. Thrives in sun or part shade.
Evergreen clematis (*Clematis armandii*)	Up to 5m (16ft)	Early spring blooms with almond-scented white flowers. Fast-growing and vigorous. Prefers sun and a sheltered spot.
Common ivy (*Hedera helix*)	Up to 10m (33ft)	Hardy, self-clinging climber with year-round foliage. Excellent for wildlife and shady areas. Tolerates poor soils and pollution.
Henry's honeysuckle (*Lonicera henryi*)	Up to 8m (26ft)	Semi-evergreen with twining stems and deep green leaves. Tubular red and yellow flowers in summer. Scented and attractive to pollinators.
Wintercreeper (*Euonymus fortunei*)	Up to 3m (10ft)	Clings to walls or trails if unsupported. Varieties with green or variegated leaves. Excellent for ground cover or low vertical greening. Tolerates shade and cold.

GARDEN FEATURES

Ⓐ Finestone stairs connect the terrace to the upper-level garden.

Ⓑ The sunken courtyard is a sheltered spot with sculptural planting.

Ⓒ Clipped boxwood (*Buxus sempervirens*) spheres in tall planters bring structure and year-round greenery.

Ⓓ The lawn offers an open contrast to the busy planting.

Ⓔ Perennial beds with fleabane (*Erigeron*) and Mexican feather grass (*Stipa tenuissima*) soften the edges.

Ⓕ A multistemmed serviceberry (*Amelanchier*) provides dappled shade.

Ⓖ The seating area is a secluded space for relaxation.

Ⓗ Vertical planting and climbers add privacy and blur the boundaries to give the illusion of a larger garden room.

Ⓘ Star jasmine adds fragrance and greenery.

Ⓙ An evergreen hedge of cherry laurel (*Prunus laurocerasu)* provides enclosure.

Ⓚ A low, clipped boxwood hedge brings a formal element.

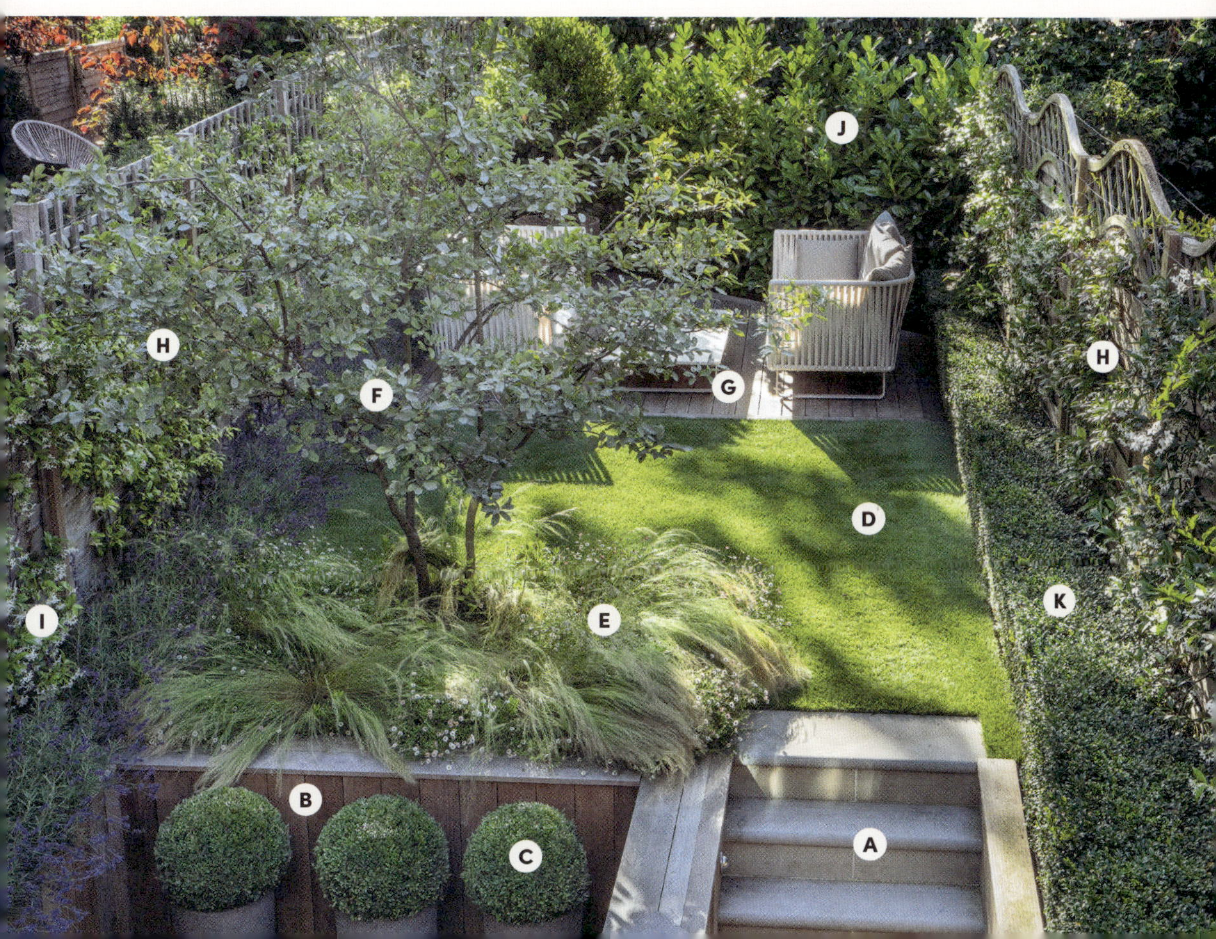

5.

Urban enclosure

Industrial-style hardware and lush plants bring this small garden to life.

This compact courtyard shows how to really make the most of limited space, and has been designed with a balance of hard and soft features, perfectly fitting in with its urban context. A Corten steel wall with an integrated shelf is the standout feature, its rusted, earthy colour complementing the surrounding greenery, and the built-in concrete bench maximizes the space available.

Concrete slabs, with low-growing plants like fleabane and mind-your-own-business in between, create a ground layer that's soft and dynamic, contrasting nicely with the otherwise hard, industrial materials. A tall birch tree adds height, its delicate leaves casting a dappled shade, while other vertical elements, including a lattice wall and evergreen climbers, help soften and enclose the space, creating a sense of seclusion.

A rusty steel drum, repurposed as a decorative feature, reinforces the garden's industrial-chic aesthetic, adding sculptural interest. Overall, the mix of natural textures, earthy materials and lush greenery transforms this small space into an intriguing retreat, proving that even the tiniest gardens can have a strong identity.

GARDEN FEATURES

(A) Corten steel is a material that works in almost any context: natural, formal, urban or rural. Its warm colour complements the cooler grey concrete tones and vivid greens.

(B) Built-in concrete bench provides integrated seating without taking up additional space.

(C) The lattice wall supports vertical plants, making optimal use of the garden's height.

(D) The reflective glass screens act like a mirror and enlarge the narrow backyard.

(E) Concrete slabs are softened by greenery.

(F) A silver birch tree (*Betula pendula*) introduces height and dappled shade, enhancing the layered structure.

(G) Fleabane (*Erigeron*) and mind-your-own-business (*Soleirolia soleirolii*) thrive in the gaps between paving.

(H) Rusty foxglove (*Digitalis ferruginea*) adds vertical interest with its tall, slender flower spikes

(I) Sedges (*Carex*) provide a textural contrast with their fine, arching leaves.

(J) Germander (*Teucrium*) thrives in dry spaces between the walls and garden, requiring minimal maintenance.

(K) Evergreen climbers soften the hard surfaces and provide year-round greenery.

Designing urban courtyards

Make the most of vertical space

When you're short on ground space, walls and fences can become part of your garden. Trellises, climbing plants and green walls can make it look lush without taking up extra space.

Choose multifunctional features

Built-in seating, wall-mounted planters and integrated lighting add functionality without taking up too much room. A bench that also works as a retaining wall can save space.

Add layers of plants to create depth

A mix of low ground covers, medium perennials and taller trees or shrubs creates depth and a feeling of abundance. For ground cover, try mind-your-own-business or creeping thyme (*Thymus serpyllum*) for a soft base. Medium perennials like lady's mantle (*Alchemilla mollis*) and Japanese anemone (*Anemone hupehenis*) offer long-season interest and gentle texture. For height and structure, consider serviceberry (*Amelanchier*) or multi-stemmed birches. Choose plants with fine textures, such as grasses or ferns, to soften hard edges and blend structural elements into the planting.

Use light colours

Light-coloured walls can reflect light and make a small space feel larger.

Frame views to extend the space

Position key features – like a striking tree or sculptural element – where they can be viewed from inside the home, making the garden feel like a natural extension of the living space.

Top Creeping thyme (*Thymus serpyllum*).
Bottom Mind-your-own-business (*Soleirolia soleirolii*).

6.

Modernist space
Reduce to the max. This minimalist garden is the perfect frame for architectural plants.

This pared-back courtyard utilizes a limited palette of materials and colours, balancing clean lines, open spaces and careful plant choices. Smooth stone slabs in grey and beige create an architectural base, while a bespoke bench has been designed to curve around a tree, bringing a feeling of movement and softening the straight lines evident throughout the rest of the scheme. The purple vertical lattice contrasts with the warm wooden cladding, adding depth and texture.

The planting is kept to a minimum and the species are carefully chosen for their architectural forms. A black bamboo adds some vertical interest, a variegated yucca is spotlit from below, providing a fabulous focal point when lit up, and a Chilean wine palm adds an exotic feel to the space.

The furniture matches the garden's modern vibe, with iconic chairs and a table that offer a sculptural focal point. The end result feels like a sanctuary of calm, and is the perfect space for outdoor entertaining.

Above Black bamboo (*Phyllostachys nigra*).

Above Spanish dagger (*Yucca gloriosa* 'Variegata').

Top five plants for architectural impact

NAME	HEIGHT	SPECIAL FEATURES
Black bamboo (*Phyllostachys nigra*)	2–3m (6–10ft)	Elegant black culms add contrast in foliage-dominated schemes. Hardy and best kept in containers to prevent spreading.
Spanish dagger (*Yucca gloriosa*)	1.5–2.5m (5–8ft)	Sword-like evergreen foliage. Some cultivars offer cream-variegated leaves for added brightness. Tolerant of drought and coastal conditions.
Tibetan cherry (*Prunus serrula*)	3–4m (10–13ft)	Ornamental tree with mahogany-coloured peeling bark. Offers spring blossom and light dappled shade. Hardy and elegant.
Chilean wine palm (*Jubaea chilensis*)	Up to 15m (50ft)	A slow-growing architectural palm with a massive grey trunk and feathery fronds. Exceptionally hardy for a subtropical palm.
Cabbage palm (*Cordyline australis*)	2–3m (6–10ft)	Spiky, upright foliage. Tolerates wind and coastal exposure. Can be grown in pots and pruned to maintain size.

GARDEN FEATURES

(A) Stone paving provides a sleek, contemporary base. Beige introduces warmth and contrasts with the cool-toned grey.

(B) A sculptural metal bench creates a sense of movement.

(C) An artificial lawn adds a touch of green while maintaining the clean aesthetic and requiring no maintenance.

(D) The purple vertical lattice provides a bold pop of colour.

(E) Horizontal wooden cladding in orange-brown tones introduces natural warmth.

(F) Black-stemmed bamboo adds height and drama.

(G) Fibreglass or polypropylene seating reflects the modern look and pairs seamlessly with the smooth surfaces.

(H) A Chilean wine palm (*Jubaea chilensis*) brings a tropical touch with its elegant fronds.

(I) An integrated spotlight adds nighttime ambiance and highlights the sculptural yucca (*Yucca gloriosa* 'Variegata').

(J) A multistemmed ornamental cherry *(Prunus)* provides seasonal interest with its striking bark and delicate spring blossoms.

7.

Shady seclusion
A shaded garden provides a welcome retreat, especially in the hot summer months.

This hidden garden is perfect for escaping the bustle of daily life. It's tucked away beneath beautiful trees like the large, towering thorny locust tree, and the formal planting scheme still maintains a naturalistic feel. Shaded gardens are all about embracing the quiet beauty of dappled light and cool, green textures. Instead of battling against the shade, plants that thrive in lower light have been chosen to create a lush, layered look.

Taller trees and shrubs such as dark red Japanese maples and privet create an overhead canopy, while mid-sized structural plants and semi-shade-tolerant grasses like feather reed grass add texture and movement, and ground-level flowering shrubs supply colour and seasonal interest.

The wooden slats extend the wall height, offering privacy while still letting in plenty of filtered sunlight. This garden feels expansive thanks to the clever use of structure and planting. The slate pathway helps define the layout, and incorporates drainage at either side. With a shaded garden, moisture is key, so regular watering in drier months and climates is essential.

GARDEN FEATURES

Ⓐ Slate paving with integrated drainage to the sides provides structure.

Ⓑ Privet (*Ligustrum*) grows light and airy when left alone and not clipped (as is usual with hedges).

Ⓒ Horizontal lattice provides privacy while allowing dappled light through.

Ⓓ Japanese maple adds deep red hues that stand out against the greenery.

Ⓔ The thorny locust tree (*Gleditsia triacanthos* 'Sunburst') filters sunlight for a soft glow. This cultivar has no thorns and is better for urban gardens than the true species. Leaves are bright yellow when young and change to a greenish-yellow later in the year.

Ⓕ Red bistort is ideal for late-season colour, ensuring visual interest into autumn.

Ⓖ Feather reed grass creates vertical structure with its tall, wafty plumes.

Ⓗ The Chinese rice-paper plant adds large, dramatic foliage that enhances the tropical feel. It can easily be kept in check by pruning, should the stems become too large.

How to plant a shaded garden

Choose surfaces that reflect light

Dark paving can make a shaded garden feel heavy, but pairing it with lighter plants and materials can stop the space from feeling too closed in. Plants soften hard surfaces and create natural flow. Opting for stone with subtle tonal variations can also help reflect available light, brightening the space even in shade. Bear in mind that stone surfaces appear much darker when wet.

Layer foliage for depth

Combining broad-leaved perennials with airy grasses creates a rich, evolving display. Plants like red bistort (*Persicaria amplexicaulis* 'Firetail') and feather reed grass (*Calamagrostis* × *acutiflora* 'Karl Foerster') add interest and subtle changes in colour.

Introduce vertical elements

In compact gardens, adding height is key to creating a feeling of enclosure without making the space feel cluttered. Lattice panels provide privacy and let in filtered light, softening the boundaries. Climbing plants trained along these structures can enhance the feeling of depth and enclosure.

Above Japanese maple (*Acer palmatum*).

Play with colour contrast

A well-balanced shade garden comes to life with contrast. Dark-leaved small trees like Japanese maple (*Acer palmatum* 'Bloodgood') make a bold statement against lighter colours, while the mix of red flowers and golden grasses adds warmth. If you pick plants with different leaf shapes and textures, the contrast stays interesting and makes the whole space look more organized.

Choose shade-tolerant plants

A lot of plants do well in low light, so the choice is huge and offers much more than ferns and hosta. Many sun-tolerant plants like bistorts and feather reed grasses are great in partial shade. Bold foliage from species such as Chinese rice-paper plant (*Tetrapanax papyrifer*) creates a more dramatic effect. A mix of textures and flowering times ensures variety throughout the seasons.

8.

Aquatic wonderland
Water gardens provide an opportunity for gentle reflection, offering a calming sensory experience.

Adding a water garden to a small courtyard brings serenity and movement without overwhelming the space. In compact gardens like this, where every element must earn its place, it offers a simple but powerful way to create atmosphere.

This enchanting courtyard garden blends sculptural design with lush Mediterranean planting including perovskias and clipped boxwood spheres, creating a space that feels both modern and organic. The reflective water basin introduces an ever-changing surface that mirrors the sky and surrounding greenery. Marsh plants such as bulrush and sedges thrive along the edges, softening the architectural lines.

The fibreglass table, bench and stools, designed to resemble raw-cut wood and tree stumps, contribute to an aesthetic that is at once rustic and contemporary. The wooden decking, with its soft grey patina, enhances the natural feel, providing warmth and texture underfoot.

A suspended lamp extends the indoor design outdoors, casting a soft glow that transforms the space after dusk. Against the walls, a striking art panel adds another layer of visual interest, while a dense hedge of Cipressino olives ensures privacy.

GARDEN FEATURES

Ⓐ The water basin introduces movement and creates a tranquil ambiance. Always consult a structural engineer when installing heavy elements on a balcony or terrace. To keep the water fresh and healthy (and keep away mosquitoes) install a small pump to circulate water.

Ⓑ A fibreglass table and seating by Gaetano Pesce add a sculptural yet organic feature.

Ⓒ The suspended lamp extends the interior design outdoors.

Ⓓ Blue star creeper (*Lobelia pedunculata*) softens the edges of the basin. It also makes it easier for insects and birds to land when they come to drink.

Ⓔ Marsh plants such as bulrush and sedges provide a contrast to the structured elements.

Ⓕ A wall art screen is an unusual background when glimpsed through the rushes.

Ⓖ Cipressino olive tree (*Olea europaea* 'Cipressino') introduces Mediterranean character. This variety is especially frost-tolerant.

Ⓗ Underplanting with busy lizzie (*Impatiens*) and stinking iris (*Iris foetidissima*) adds seasonal colour.

Ⓘ Russian sage (*Salvia yangii* syn. *Perovskia atriplicifolia*) adds both colour and fragrance.

Ⓙ Clipped boxwood (*Buxus sempervirens*) spheres lend a structured, classical element.

Above Yellow flag Iris (*Iris pseudacorus*).

Above Horsetail (*Equisetum hyemale*).

Top five plants for water basins

NAME	WATER DEPTH	SPECIAL FEATURES
Water lily (*Nymphaea*)	30–90cm (12–35in)	Floating leaves and flowers, doesn't like moving water. Needs still water and full sun.
Bulrush, cattail (*Typha* spp.)	5–20cm (2–8in)	Slender vertical stems, ideal for small water basins. Easy to grow in shallow water. May need thinning to control spread.
Yellow flag Iris (*Iris pseudacorus*)	10–30cm (4–12in)	Bold yellow flowers. Thrives in damp soils and shallow water. Tough and low maintenance but can spread so best in contained beds.
Horsetail (*Equisetum hyemale*)	5–15cm (2–6in)	Architectural evergreen stems. Prefers shallow margins. Vigorous grower.
Water soldier (*Stratiotes aloides*)	20–50cm (8–20in)	Floating rosettes sink in winter. Oxygenates water and supports wildlife. No planting needed, very low maintenance.

9.

Planted pergola

Frame outdoor spaces beautifully, incorporating support for climbing plants and shade from sunlight.

A pergola isn't just an aesthetic choice – it can help to shape space and create atmosphere in a compact garden. This sophisticated pergola, made from warm-toned teak, introduces structure and subtle geometry. Its simple lines create a defined space without fully enclosing it, offering filtered light and providing support for climbing plants. In small spaces, the vertical dimension is essential, and a pergola helps draw the eye upwards, making the garden feel taller and more expansive.

Beneath the pergola, a shaded dining nook features a robust teak table and chairs whose look will only improve with age, and is framed by lush planting that softens the structure. A Yorkstone terrace defines the elevated seating area, the paving speckled with low-growing plants like bellflowers and fleabane, which spill from the cracks between stones and add an overgrown, romantic charm.

Fragrant Mediterranean container plants, including lemon and olive trees, add structure and keep things interesting throughout the season, reinforcing the warm, natural palette. Carefully clipped evergreens like yew frame the space, making it feel refined.

Designing with pergolas

Placing your pergola

Thoughtfully siting a pergola ensures it becomes a natural extension of your living space. A pergola should feel proportionate to the garden, offering shade without overwhelming the space. Position it near the house for easy access to outdoor dining, or nestle it deeper into the garden to create a destination retreat. South-facing pergolas offer the most sun, ideal for heat-loving climbers, while east-facing structures provide gentle morning light and afternoon shade. Ensure good air circulation to maintain an airy feel and prevent mildew on foliage, and consider surrounding plantings to frame the view or screen less attractive areas.

Choose durable materials

Opt for hardwoods such as oak or teak, or consider metal for a more contemporary look. Longevity and weather resistance are key considerations.

Maximize functionality

Use the pergola as more than just a decorative feature – integrate lighting, hanging lanterns or outdoor heating for evening ambiance. Adding climbing plants or fabric canopies enhances protection from sun and light rain, ensuring comfort year-round.

Choose the right climbers

Wisteria, climbing roses or star jasmine (*Trachelospermum jasminoides*) are classic choices for pergolas, offering seasonal scent and cascading flower displays. Choose twining climbers like clematis or honeysuckle (*Lonicera* spp.) for rapid vertical coverage and visual drama. For a more contemporary look, common ivy (*Hedera helix*), climbing hydrangea (*Hydrangea petiolaris*) or the vigorous *Clematis armandii* provide lush foliage all year.

Where space allows, trailing plants like nasturtiums (*Tropaeolum majus*) or sweet peas (*Lathyrus odoratus*) can spill from hanging planters or climb support wires, adding delicate movement and fragrance. For edible appeal, grapevines (*Vitis vinifera*) and passionflowers (*Passiflora caerulea*) offer seasonal interest and provide delicious fruit.

Right Fleabane (*Erigeron karvinskianus*).

GARDEN FEATURES

(A) Yorkstone paving lends a timeless elegance while providing durability and character.

(B) Sturdy teak outdoor furniture will weather beautifully over time.

(C) The pergola supports climbing plants such as wisteria, while providing shelter and shade. Here, the pergola and dining set are made of the same wood – sturdy and long-lasting teak – creating a coherent look. Don't treat teak that is exposed to the elements with oil or varnish as this will result in an endless cycle of care. It is better to let the wood age and develop a patina.

(D) Fleabane (*Erigeron karvinskianus)* grows in the paving cracks, creating a soft, naturalistic effect.

(E) Bellflowers (*Campanula)* add some delicate seasonal colour.

(F) Clipped evergreens such as yew *(Taxus baccata)* provide year-round structure.

(G) Mediterranean container plants, including lemons and olives, introduce a warm, southern European vibe.

(H) A carefully curated planting scheme, including herbs such as lavender, softens the edges of the patio.

10.

Wildlife haven

Even in a small and confined place, you can create a wildlife-friendly garden.

The smallest of gardens has the potential to support wildlife. In this compact plot, a thoughtful planting scheme, water feature and clever habitat creation form a welcoming environment for pollinators, birds, amphibians and beneficial insects. Far from requiring wild or unkempt corners, a wildlife-friendly garden can be neat, colourful and highly ornamental – while still playing an important ecological role.

At the heart of this design is a small, stone-edged pond. Though modest in size, it quickly becomes a magnet for life: frogs and newts find refuge among the marginal plants, while insects and birds visit to drink and bathe. Around it, planting is densely layered and deliberately varied, combining ornamental grasses, nectar-rich perennials like ornamental alliums and small flowering shrubs.

Structures like open paving joints and climbing frames allow both movement and shelter for a range of species. Potted plants – some seasonal, some permanent – add further diversity and microhabitats. A paved seating corner offers a place to quietly observe the activity all around. This is a garden where beauty and biodiversity work hand in hand, proving that a wildlife haven can flourish in even the most confined plot.

GARDEN FEATURES

Ⓐ A pond is key for biodiversity, supporting frogs, insects and birds.

Ⓑ A mix of perennials and shrubs attracts a range of insects and birds.

Ⓒ Alliums (*Allium hollandicum*) provide food with their nectar-rich globes.

Ⓓ Stepping stones with open joints encourage moss and creeping plants, and allow wildlife movement.

Ⓔ Climbers such as star jasmine (*Trachelospermum jasminoides*) and climbing roses provide both nectar and shelter.

Ⓕ Bronze elder offers both flowers and berries for birds and insects.

Ⓖ An open fence lets hedgehogs and other creatures travel between gardens.

Ⓗ Potted plants create small habitat patches and can be moved or grouped for seasonal effect.

Ⓘ An unobtrusive seating area is a quiet spot to observe the surrounding wildlife in action.

Supporting wildlife in small spaces

Start with water

A pond, however small, is one of the most effective features for increasing biodiversity. Still water supports frogs, insects and birds, and quickly becomes a thriving mini-ecosystem. Even a buried container or shallow basin can make a difference.

Diversity is key

The more plant types and structures you include, the more species your garden will attract. Combine evergreen shrubs, nectar-rich flowers, grasses and seed heads to create a continuous cycle of food and shelter.

Favour native species – but not exclusively

Native plants are essential for local insect life, but well-chosen exotics can extend flowering times and provide pollen when native plants are not in flower. For example, combine early-summer flowering European ox-eye daisies (*Leucanthemum vulgare*) with North American coneflowers (*Echinacea* and *Rudbeckia*), which bloom later in the season. You can also use ornamental selections of native species like the bronze-leaved and pink flowering elder (*Sambucus nigra* 'Black Lace') instead of the ordinary species.

Keep movement and permeability

Use stepping stones with gaps for moss and creeping plants. Avoid hard boundaries: open fences or hedges allow animals like hedgehogs to pass through, while trellis and climbers add vertical habitat.

Above Ox eye daisy (*Leucanthemum vulgare*).

Make room for structure

Taller plants like shrubs or small trees offer nesting spots, shade and height variation. Deciduous species contribute to the seasonal rhythm and provide leaf litter for overwintering insects.

Observe and adapt

A small seating area lets you watch wildlife up close and notice how the garden evolves through the seasons. Add habitat features as you go, like log piles, nesting habitats for wild bees (insect hotels) or shallow dishes for water.

Multipurpose gardens with ideas for edible growing, safe play areas, cosy seating, easy maintenance and year-round enjoyment.

PRACTICAL SPACES

1.

Family garden

Eat, play, learn: repeat. This small garden offers something for all members of the family.

This cleverly designed garden blends decorative features, functionality and seasonal colour, creating an inviting outdoor space that's well suited for both rest and activity. Zoning the garden allows for optimization of the small space, with distinct areas for dining, playing and growing.

A lawned area provides an open and versatile green space for safe tumbling or stretching out and relaxing, while a raised terrace defines an outdoor seating area that's perfect for picnics and parties. The robust table, bench and chairs are scattered with colourful cushions that pick out the hues of the surrounding hydrangeas.

A backdrop of sculptural evergreens are low-maintenance and provide year-round greenery. The elevated terrace, which is almost like a treehouse, extends the usable space upwards and can be utilized as a fun play fort or fairy castle. It also integrates a useful storage area for gardening equipment and cushions.

Vegetables thrive in raised beds, providing a productive use of the space and a fun opportunity to make gardening a family activity and teach children about growing, nature and sustainability.

What to include in a family garden

Flexible, multifunctional spaces

A family garden should adapt to changing needs, from imaginative play to quiet reading or hosting friends. Divide the garden into zones: open lawns for games, shaded corners for rest, and raised beds for learning to grow food.

Low-maintenance planting

Incorporate a diverse selection of native plants, including perennials, grasses, shrubs and trees that thrive in your local climate and soil conditions. Native plants tend to require less maintenance.

Interesting hardscaping

Use natural materials such as stone, wood and gravel to create paths, borders and structures. Incorporate fun elements like stepping stones and balance beams made from dead wood, create a tree fort or hang a rope swing from a sturdy tree.

Encourage biodiversity

Provide habitat and food sources for wildlife. Add bird feeders, nesting boxes and bee hotels, or create a butterfly garden. Foster a thriving ecosystem and children will be able to observe birds, bugs and blooms up close. Kit them out with a magnifying glass and notebook for hours of outdoor entertainment.

Above Cosmea (*Cosmos bipinnatuus*).

Year-round interest

Select plants that offer seasonal blooms, foliage colour and textural variation. Incorporate a mix of early-spring bulbs, summer-flowering perennials and autumn grasses to create a dynamic landscape that delights the senses throughout the year. For additional autumn interest, add late-flowering prairie and steppe perennials like echinaceas, asters or salvias.

Pet-safe planting

If your garden is shared with pets, choose non-toxic plants and avoid common hazards like lilies, foxgloves or euphorbias. Instead, opt for safe options like marigolds (*Calendula*), rosemary or snapdragons (*Antirrhinum*). Always check before planting, and provide shaded rest areas and a clean water source to keep animals cool and comfortable outdoors.

GARDEN FEATURES

(A) A lawned play area offers a soft, open space for recreation and relaxation.

(B) An elevated terrace establishes a defined dining and social area.

(C) Dark pink cosmea (*Cosmos bipinnatus*) thrive in pots and add seasonal colour.

(D) Sculptural evergreens like these laurels (*Laurus nobilis*) form a structured, year-round backdrop and supply the kitchen with aromatic leaves.

(E) An elevated play area provides a fun, dedicated play space for children.

(F) Raised beds are ideal for growing vegetables and herbs. The wooden frames are set in gravel, which enhances their longevity as there is no direct contact of wood with the soil. Here fennel, nasturtiums, kale and runner beans wait to be harvested. Later in the year, chard and lettuce add nutritious variety.

(G) A small pear tree bears its first fruits.

(H) Rhododendrons are surprisingly robust and can withstand the occasional rough handling during kids' ball games.

2.

Eco-friendly hub

A sustainable space with thoughtful planting and design details that both humans and wildlife will enjoy.

This neat garden combines ecological and functional elements. Defined by distinct zones, the layout maximizes the limited space. A lawned play area provides an open, soft surface for recreation, ensuring a dedicated space for children without compromising the design.

The integrated wooden bench offers a practical seating solution, and the neutral grey-blue fence grounds the design and is softened by climbing plants that add seasonal variation. The multifunctional garden shed provides space for storage and play, its green roof planted with succulents like stonecrop reinforcing the garden's commitment to biodiversity by supporting pollinators.

Beyond its aesthetic appeal, the planting scheme has a practical purpose. Herbs and perennials like purple top (*Verbena bonariensis*), rosemary and alliums in containers lend fragrance and texture while attracting beneficial insects. Potted plants offer flexibility and allow for seasonal adjustments. The densely planted borders and green walls offer retreats and nesting areas for a variety of wildlife, from insects to birds, hedgehogs and shrews. Serviceberries (*Amelanchier*) bordering the terrace provide nectar and food for wildlife with their spring flowers and berries in late summer.

GARDEN FEATURES

Ⓐ Even a small lawn helps cool an area, reducing heat compared to paving or decking.

Ⓑ The wooden bench is both a seating area and structural divide.

Ⓒ Designed to evolve with family needs, this garden house can begin as a children's hideaway, then transition into a shed or quiet studio. The planted roof adds to the eco-value of the garden.

Ⓓ A close-boarded fence in neutral grey-blue provides enclosure.

Ⓔ Racks offer practical storage solutions, keeping tools, accessories and firewood organized.

Ⓕ Climbers like star jasmine (*Trachelospermum jasminoides*) soften the fence.

Ⓖ A herb and perennial bed introduces scent and biodiversity.

Ⓗ A green roof provides insulation and supports pollinators.

Ⓘ Slate brick divides the terrace and lawn and is easy to maintain.

Ⓙ The terrace defines the dining area and connects the garden with the house.

Ⓚ Potted plants bring flexibility, allowing for seasonal updates.

Create an eco-friendly garden

Above Stonecrop (*Sedum*) planted on a green roof.

Use sustainably sourced materials

Incorporate wood, stone or gravel that has been responsibly harvested or recycled. These materials not only reduce environmental impact but also age beautifully, blending into the garden's aesthetic while reducing the need for frequent replacement or treatment.

Embrace diverse, wildlife-friendly planting

A mix of flowering perennials, native shrubs and grasses ensures food and shelter for beneficial insects, birds and other animals throughout the year. Diversity also helps create a more resilient garden that can better withstand pests, diseases and changing weather.

Consider a green roof

Living roofs help regulate temperature, manage rainwater run-off and offer additional habitat for insects. They also add visual interest from above and soften built structures like sheds or studios, integrating them into the garden.

Prioritize native and layered vegetation

Native species are adapted to local conditions, often requiring less water and maintenance. Planting in layers – using ground covers, mid-height perennials and taller shrubs – mimics natural ecosystems, improves soil health and offers year-round interest. Bare soil is not a natural state, so cover the ground with plants or mulch as this will prevent weeds from germinating and reduces evaporation, making maintenance easier.

Introduce flexible shading options

Retractable sails or fabric canopies allow you to adjust for the seasons, providing shade on hot summer days. This not only improves comfort for garden users but also protects sensitive plants from excessive sun exposure.

3.

Fun and versatile
This functional garden demonstrates how a well-designed outdoor space can work across all generations.

This garden is the perfect place for kids and grown-ups to play, relax and enjoy family activities. It's all about having dedicated areas for different things, such as a play area with a sand box and a playhouse, a dining space, a lawn for playing games and a decked terrace where adults can enjoy a morning coffee or an evening aperitif.

Edible gardening is a big deal here, with raised beds bursting with tomatoes, herbs and vegetables, letting the kids get their hands dirty and experience the joy of growing their own food. The garden is enclosed by a wooden fence that not only creates a sense of seclusion but also incorporates integrated planters for climbers, perennials and ornamental grasses, adding softness and movement to the structure.

There's a raised seating area with a built-in bench and dining table, which is a great spot for outdoor meals and can also be used to keep an eye on the play and planting areas. The design is well thought-out, combining functionality with natural beauty, and the result is a harmonious space where the whole family can connect with nature and each other.

Above Sugar snap pea (*Pisum sativum* 'Sugar Snap').

Above Radish (*Raphanus sativus*).

Fruit and veg for gardening fun

NAME	SEASON	SPECIAL FEATURES
Cherry tomatoes	Summer	Easy to pick, sweet taste and grow in small spaces; select colourful varieties like yellow or orange alongside red for extra fun.
Carrots	Spring–autumn	Fun to pull from the soil, and make a naturally sweet and healthy garden snack.
Sugar snap peas	Spring–autumn	Sweet and crunchy, these are edible straight from the plant, no peeling required; add a small trellis for them to climb.
Strawberries	Summer	Easy to grow in containers or beds; choose everbearing varieties for a longer harvest season.
Radishes	Spring–autumn	Quick to grow (can be ready in about 3–4 weeks) so perfect for impatient young gardeners; choose mild varieties to ensure they're child-friendly.

GARDEN FEATURES

- (A) A small lawn provides a soft surface for tumbling.
- (B) Play zone for younger children. Sand can easily be swept from the wooden decking.
- (C) Built-in storage ensures that toys and garden essentials remain neatly tucked away.
- (D) A discreet seating area is a more intimate space for quiet moments.
- (E) Raised beds allow for easy edible gardening. Engage little gardeners by planting a pizza plot with tomatoes, basil, peppers and garlic.
- (F) A raised seating area subtly defines different sections of the garden.
- (G) A large dining table with a custom-built bench maximizes seating capacity for family meals.
- (H) Wooden fence integrates planting for climbers, grasses and perennials.
- (I) Vegetables, such as courgettes, are grown on the roof, maximizing the space.
- (J) A small cherry tree provides sweet fruits for snacking. It can be easily kept in check by pruning.
- (K) Fragrant, touch-friendly plants like these scented pelargoniums enhance the sensory experience.

Outdoor kitchen

This stylish garden proves that outdoor spaces can be both highly functional and beautifully designed.

This multifunctional garden is perfect for relaxed outdoor dining, with a fully equipped kitchen and a lush, productive planting scheme. The space is designed around a large wooden dining table with bench seating, and the kitchen zone utilizes weather-resistant stainless steel and has a built-in grill, sink and plenty of storage.

A rust-coloured wall defines the outdoor kitchen, doubling as a privacy screen and a functional storage area, with shelves for utensils and fresh herbs. The warm tone of the wall is echoed in the raised planting beds, which create a structured planting scheme.

The garden itself is full of ornamental and edible planting, blending flowers, herbs and vegetables in a vibrant, naturalistic arrangement. The raised beds and upcycled zinc containers not only look great, but they're also practical, making sure there are always fresh ingredients on hand for cooking. The integrated lighting means the garden can be enjoyed after dark, creating a cosy, relaxed atmosphere.

GARDEN FEATURES

Ⓐ Sturdy outdoor furniture is ideal to host the whole family. A bench is versatile and seats more than individual chairs.

Ⓑ The outdoor kitchen is positioned adjacent to the indoor kitchen for maximum flexibility. Both kitchens can be used simultaneously when the sliding door is open.

Ⓒ A fixed back wall allows for shelves for storing accessories and crockery.

Ⓓ Ornamental plants like iris and leopard plant (*Ligularia dentata*) in custom-built raw steel raised beds bring seasonal texture and encourage biodiversity.

Ⓔ Upcycled containers made from zinc buckets provide additional growing space.

Ⓕ Integrated raised beds positioned along the steps help retain soil while visually connecting the different levels of the garden.

Ⓖ A large raised bed for perennials and small shrubs like crocosmias, catmint and salvias softens the edges of the space and adds structure.

Plan an outdoor kitchen

Built-in grill

The grill is the heart of an outdoor kitchen. Choose one with integrated housing and a fitted lid to shield it from wind and rain. Stainless steel is durable, rust-resistant and easy to clean. Position the grill where cooking smoke will dissipate easily, ideally with overhead clearance and airflow.

Sink and water access

A sink is useful, especially if you're not very close to the house. If plumbing isn't available, consider a gravity-fed water container or connect a hose with a quick-coupling system.

Work surface

Stone, tiles or steel surfaces are best suited to withstand heat, weather and spills. Place prep zones close to the grill for efficiency. A deep ledge can also double as a buffet surface.

Smart storage

Include drawers or cabinets with weatherproof finishes to store essentials. Open shelving for potted herbs or baskets of fruit adds charm, and hooks and rails can also be used to hang frequently used tools.

Power and gas connections

An outdoor socket allows you to plug in appliances like a blender or electric grill, while task lighting above the workspace ensures functionality after dark. For frequent use, a built-in gas line removes the need for portable bottles.

Grow herbs where you cook

Planter boxes or zinc containers filled with aromatic herbs like rosemary, thyme and lemon balm (*Melissa officinalis*) offer ingredients at arm's reach, and also deter mosquitoes and scent the air.

Durability and ease of maintenance

Every element in an outdoor kitchen must be weather-resistant, from flooring to furniture. Use paving that's easy to sweep and clean: natural stone, composite decking or outdoor porcelain tiles work well.

Right Rosemary (*Salvia rosmarinus*).

5.

Veggie plot

A garden that is literally good enough to eat, offering an (almost) year-round bounty of fresh produce.

An edible garden can be every bit as pretty as a traditional flower garden. This veggie patch is both productive and beautiful, and has been carefully designed to have a natural feel. Raised wooden beds flank the dining area and provide the best conditions for growing a variety of vegetables and herbs, and the high hedge offers protection from the elements.

The warm-toned timber beds match the wooden storage units of the outdoor kitchen and support a range of crops, from leafy greens to root vegetables. Mediterranean herbs do well in the gravelled spaces between stepping stones. Perennial plantings add ornamental interest, soften the edges of the paved seating area and attract beneficial insects that help keep pests in check.

To enhance its visual appeal, the garden makes use of a multi-height planting scheme, combining low herbs, medium vegetables and tall hedges and climbers on trellises for privacy. Colour is introduced through both flowers and decorative foliage, while painted chairs add an easy charm. Trellises create vertical accents and support climbers like star jasmine, which fills the area with a beautiful scent.

Gardening in raised beds

Above Chard (*Beta vulgaris* 'Ruby Chard').

Saves time and effort

Raised beds eliminate the need for heavy digging, reduce weeds and make harvesting easier. They provide a comfortable height to lean on when gardening and are less of a strain for those with mobility challenges.

Customized growing conditions

You have more control and can fill them with a soil mix tailored to what you are growing, resulting in faster growth, larger leaves and stronger roots.

Natural pest control

Many pests, such as vegetable flies, rarely fly higher than 50cm (20in), so raised beds help protect crops from infestation. They also help protect against crawling pests such as slugs and snails.

Longer growing season

Because the soil in raised beds warms quickly in spring and can be covered in autumn, they allow for earlier planting and later harvesting.

Where to site

Choose a location that receives at least six hours of sunlight per day, especially if you plan to grow vegetables, fruits or Mediterranean herbs. Place close to the house for easy access and frequent harvesting, ideally near a water source. Ensure the site is level and has good drainage, as standing water at the base of the bed can undermine plant health.

Best materials to build

Opt for untreated hardwoods like oak, larch or cedar, which are naturally resistant to decay. Avoid chemically treated wood, which can leach into the soil. Corten steel or galvanized metal offer longevity and a contemporary edge.

Filling your bed

Start with a base layer of coarse organic matter such as twigs, branches or shredded garden waste to aid drainage. Add a layer of compost, then top it off with your soil mix. For vegetables, use a blend of loam-based soil, compost and horticultural grit. For Mediterranean herbs, use a sandy, free-draining mix. Maintain at least 30–45cm (12–18in) of soil depth for most crops, and up to 60cm (2ft) for deep-rooted vegetables like tomatoes or carrots. Mulch the surface with straw to retain moisture and suppress weeds.

GARDEN FEATURES

(A) The paved area provides a space for dining.

(B) A tall hedge offers shelter from wind and sun.

(C) Custom-built wooden storage keeps gardening tools neatly tucked away.

(D) Raised beds encircle the seating area, giving the garden a clean, contemporary look.

(E) Vegetables such as kohlrabi thrive in the well-draining, nutrient-rich soil of the raised beds.

(F) Carrots do well in the deep soil. Growing them at heights above 60cm (2ft) keeps them out of reach of carrot flies that could harm the roots.

(G) Multicoloured chard can be harvested for months. There are many different cultivars with white, green, red, yellow, orange and violet stems.

(H) Perennial plantings with geraniums, bugloss and ferns attract beneficial insects that help with pest control.

(I) Stepping stones in warm sandstone create an informal pathway for easy access between planting areas.

(J) Mediterranean herbs like thyme flourish in the gravelled spaces between stones.

Family courtyard

A clever design makes the most of this urban garden, transforming it into a practical and stylish retreat.

Despite the limited size, this courtyard garden feels remarkably spacious thanks to its clever zoning, use of levels and consistent materials.

A warm timber deck defines the main living area and creates a smooth transition from indoors to out. At mid-level, a generous dining area is shaded by a louvred pergola, while below, a smaller lawn space offers room for children to play.

Lush greenery provides softness and structure throughout. Tall bamboo, clipped evergreen shapes and a medlar tree offer privacy without enclosing the garden, while flowering climbers (such as star jasmine and kiwi) scramble across pergolas and fences, adding seasonal beauty and scent.

The design prioritises adaptability and ease of use, with built-in seating, concealed storage and durable surfaces that withstand family life. Bold yet balanced planting ensures year-round interest, while a green roof atop the shed introduces an additional layer of texture and biodiversity. The result is a garden that works hard for its scale – accommodating play, rest, dining and greenery in perfect harmony.

Zoning and levels for everyday life

Zoning through structure

This clever layout avoids the need for walls or fences by using height, surface material and planting to divide the garden into distinct areas. Raised timber decks mark the lounge and dining zone, while a lower section with lawn invites play. Generous planters and pergolas act as soft boundaries, creating a space that feels both open and defined, but offers the necessary sense of privacy.

Compact but multifunctional

Every element in this garden performs more than one role. Built-in planters with broad edges double as temporary seating, vertical supports are used for climbers and shading, and the storage shed supports a climbing frame. These multifunctional features reduce visual clutter and allow a rich diversity of uses within a small footprint.

Child-friendly by design

Designed with everyday family life in mind, the garden offers a safe environment for children without sacrificing elegance. The soft, level lawn area is perfect for games and barefoot play, while the climbing structure is tucked cleverly into a quiet corner – close enough for supervision, yet clearly zoned as a space of its own.

Smart transitions

Gentle changes in level are handled with broad timber steps that signal shifts in function while preserving flow. These subtle transitions help the garden feel generous and connected, guiding movement through the space while adding structure and rhythm overall.

Above Japanese roof iris (*Iris tectorum*).

Green as backdrop

Lush, textural planting surrounds the space on every side. Tall bamboo, clipped evergreens and broad-leaved perennials provide privacy, soften boundaries and enhance the sense of enclosure. The green palette is unified and understated, allowing key seasonal highlights – such as white blossom or bronze foliage – to take centre stage at just the right moment.

GARDEN FEATURES

(A) A timber deck defines the outdoor living space, extending the feel of the interior into the garden.

(B) Foldable reclining chairs with textile covers offer a flexible seating option.

(C) Raised beds defined planting zones and double as informal seating.

(D) Timber steps allow for subtle height changes.

(E) A generous table sits beneath a pergola, ideal for outdoor meals and shaded relaxation.

(F) Kiwis weave through the pergola, adding shade in summer.

(G) A compact shed houses tools while integrating a climbing frame, blending utility with playful design.

(H) The roof is planted with drought-tolerant sedum, providing ecological value.

(I) Green borders with climbing jasmine.

(J) Tall clumps of arrow bamboo add drama and height as well as creating privacy.

(K) Jungle like Hydrangeas, African lilies and large-leaved perennials like Japanese roof irises fill the planters evoke a lush, immersive feel.

(L) A small medlar tree with sculptural form and seasonal character– white blossom, bronze foliage and ornamental fruit – completes the planting.

What to Grow Where

You'll find most of these species mentioned in this book, and when grouped into themed lists they become a handy guide for finding the right plant for your garden. The climate zone shown next to each one is explained in the panel opposite.

Architectural plants

Cordyline (cabbage palm), ZONE 9–11
Dicksonia antarctica (soft tree fern), ZONE 9–10
Fatsia japonica (Japanese aralia), ZONE 8–10
Jubaea chilensis (Chilean wine palm), ZONE 8–10
Paulownia (princess tree), ZONE 5–9
Phormium (New Zealand flax), ZONE 8–10
Phyllostachys nigra (black bamboo), ZONE 7–10
Tetrapanax papyrifer (Chinese rice-paper plant), ZONE 7–10
Trachycarpus fortunei (Chinese windmill palm), ZONE 7–11
Yucca gloriosa 'Variegata' (variegated Spanish dagger), ZONE 7–10

Plants for a tropical look

Aralia elata (angelica tree), ZONE 4–9
Dicksonia antarctica (soft tree fern), ZONE 9–10
Fatsia japonica (Japanese aralia), ZONE 8–10
Hakonechloa macra (hakone grass), ZONE 5–9
Hedychium densiflorum (ginger lily), ZONE 8–10
Jubaea chilensis (Chilean wine palm), ZONE 8–10
Musa basjoo (hardy banana), ZONE 7–10
Paulownia (princess tree), ZONE 6–10
Tetrapanax papyrifer (Chinese rice-paper plant), ZONE 7–10
Trachycarpus fortunei (Chinese windmill palm), ZONE 7–11

Evergreen climbers

Clematis armandii (evergreen clematis), ZONE 7–9
Euonymus fortunei (wintercreeper), ZONE 5–9
Hedera helix (common ivy), ZONE 4–9
Lonicera henryi (Henry's honeysuckle), ZONE 6–9
Mahonia (Oregon grape), ZONE 5–9
Pittosporum tobira (Japanese pittosporum), ZONE 8–10
Trachelospermum jasminoides (star jasmine), ZONE 8–10
Viburnum tinus (laurustinus), ZONE 8–10
Vinca minor (lesser periwinkle), ZONE 4–9

Long-flowering perennials

Anemone hupehensis (Japanese anemone), ZONE 4–8
Coreopsis (tickseed), ZONE 4–9
Echinacea (coneflower), ZONE 3–9
Geranium 'Rozanne' (cranesbill), ZONE 5–8
Knautia (knautia), ZONE 5–9
Nepeta (catmint), ZONE 4–8
Oenothera lindheimeri (gaura), ZONE 5–9
Rudbeckia hirta (black-eyed Susan), ZONE 3–9
Salvia nemorosa (Balkan clary), ZONE 4–8
Verbena bonariensis (purple top), ZONE 7–11

Plants for wildlife

Allium (ornamental onion), ZONE 5–8
Amelanchier (serviceberry), ZONE 4–9
Cornus sanguinea (common dogwood), ZONE 5–7
Crataegus monogyna (hawthorn), ZONE 4–7
Digitalis purpurea (foxglove), ZONE 4–8
Echinacea (coneflower), ZONE 3–9
Eupatorium cannabinum (hemp agrimony), ZONE 6–9
Lavandula angustifolia (English lavender), ZONE 5–9
Rosa (Rose), ZONE 4–9
Salvia nemorosa (Balkan clary), ZONE 4–8

Safe plants for kids

Allium (ornamental onion), ZONE 5–8
Calendula officinalis (pot marigold), ZONE 2–11
Fragaria (strawberry), ZONE 4–9
Lactuca sativa (lettuce), ZONE 4–9
Lavandula angustifolia (English lavender), ZONE 5–9
Melissa officinalis (lemon balm), ZONE 4–9
Nepeta (catmint), ZONE 4–8
Rosmarinus officinalis (rosemary), ZONE 8–10
Thymus (thyme), ZONE 5–9
Vicia faba (broad bean), ZONE 6–9

Groundcover plants

Ajuga reptans (bugleweed), ZONE 3–10
Alchemilla mollis (lady's mantle), ZONE 3–8
Brunnera macrophylla (Siberian bugloss), ZONE 3–8
Carex (sedge), ZONE 4–9*
Hosta (plantain lily), ZONE 3–9
Lamium galeobdolon (yellow archangel), ZONE 4–8
Polygonatum odoratum (Solomon's seal), ZONE 4–8
Soleirolia soleirolii (mind-your-own-business), ZONE 9–11
Thymus serpyllum (creeping thyme), ZONE 4–8
Vinca minor (lesser periwinkle), ZONE 4–9

HARDINESS ZONES

This system is used to classify regions based on their average minimum winter temperatures, helping gardeners determine which plants are likely to thrive in a specific area. Most of the featured gardens in this book are suitable for USDA zones Z7 to Z10.

Developed by the United States Department of Agriculture (USDA), these zones are widely used in North America to reflect new conditions with the changing climate. They are divided into 13 zones, based on the average annual extreme minimum winter temperature, each spanning 5.6°C (10°F) and further divided into 'a' and 'b' subzones, each representing a 2.8°C (5°F) range.

The European system of hardiness zones is adapted from the USDA Hardiness Zone Map, but modified to suit European climates. Europe's system is not officially standardized across all countries, but many gardeners refer to the Royal Horticultural Society (RHS) zones or adapted versions of the USDA zones for Europe.

For more information and detailed maps visit:

→ planthardiness.ars.usda.gov/
→ plantagreenhouses.eu/blogs/planting-zones
→ gardeningknowhow.com/planting-zones
→ gardeningknowhow.com/planting-zones/uk-hardiness-zones.htm

Key to the zones
Z1 below -45.6°C (-50°F)
Z2 -45.6°C to -40°C (-50°F to -40°F)
Z3 -40°C to -34.4°C (-40°F to -30°F)
Z4 -34.4°C to -28.9°C (-30°F to -20°F)
Z5 -28.9°C to -23.3°C (-20°F to -10°F)
Z6 -23.3°C to -17.8°C (-10°F to 0°F)
Z7 -17.8°C to -12.2°C (0°F to 10°F)
Z8 -12.2°C to -6.7°C (10°F to 20°F)
Z9 -6.7°C to -1.1°C (20°F to 30°F)
Z10 -1.1°C to 4.4°C (30°F to 40°F)
Z11 4.4°C to 10°C (40°F to 50°F)
Z12 10°C to 15.6°C (50°F to 60°F)
Z13 above 15.6°C (60°F)

Shrubs for privacy

Buxus sempervirens (boxwood), ZONE 5–9
Cornus sanguinea (common dogwood), ZONE 5–7
Fagus sylvatica (European beech), ZONE 5–7
Laurus nobilis (bay laurel), ZONE 8–10
Ligustrum (privet), ZONE 5–8
Mahonia (Oregon grape), ZONE 5–9
Osmanthus (osmanthus), ZONE 7–10
Prunus laurocerasus (cherry laurel), ZONE 6–9
Taxus baccata (English yew), ZONE 6–8
Viburnum tinus (laurustinus), ZONE 8–10

Plants for dry shade

Asplenium scolopendrium (hart's-tongue fern), ZONE 4–9
Brunnera macrophylla (Siberian bugloss), ZONE 3–8
Epimedium × *perralchicum* (barrenwort), ZONE 5–8
Fatsia japonica (Japanese aralia), ZONE 8–10
Helleborus (hellebore), ZONE 4–9
Mahonia (Oregon grape), ZONE 5–9
Polystichum setiferum (soft shield fern), ZONE 5–8
Sarcococca (sweet box), ZONE 6–9
Vinca minor (lesser periwinkle), ZONE 4–9
Euonymus fortunei (wintercreeper), ZONE 5–9

Wildflower meadow plants

Achillea (yarrow), ZONE 3–9
Campanula (bellflower), ZONE 3–8
Centaurea (knapweed/cornflower), ZONE 3–9
Daucus carota (wild carrot), ZONE 3–8
Knautia (knautia), ZONE 5–9
Leucanthemum (ox-eye Daisy), ZONE 4–8
Sanguisorba (burnet), ZONE 4–8
Scabiosa (scabious), ZONE 4–8
Silene vulgaris (red campion), ZONE 4–8
Trifolium (clover), ZONE 3–9

Scheme for a sunny patio

Agapanthus (African lily), ZONE 6–10
Eryngium (sea holly), ZONE 4–9
Lavandula angustifolia (English lavender), ZONE 5–9
Nepeta (catmint), ZONE 4–8
Perovskia (Russian sage), ZONE 4–9
Salvia nemorosa (Balkan clary), ZONE 4–8
Santolina chamaecyparissus (lavender cotton), ZONE 6–9
Sedum spp. (stonecrop), ZONE 4–9
Stipa tenuissima (Mexican feather grass), ZONE 7–10
Verbena bonariensis (purple top), ZONE 7–11

Sensory plants

Lavandula angustifolia (English lavender), ZONE 5–9
Melissa officinalis (lemon balm), ZONE 4–9
Mentha (mint), ZONE 3–11
Nepeta (catmint), ZONE 4–8
Pelargonium (scented pelargonium), ZONE 10–11
Rosmarinus officinalis (rosemary), ZONE 8–10
Salvia nemorosa (Balkan clary), ZONE 4–8
Salvia officinalis (common sage), ZONE 5–9
Santolina chamaecyparissus (Lavender cotton), ZONE 6–9
Thymus (thyme), ZONE 5–9

Drought-tolerant plants

Achillea (yarrow), ZONE 3–9
Ballota pseudodictamnus (false dittany), ZONE 7–10
Cistus × *purpureus* (orchid rock rose), ZONE 8–10
Eryngium (sea holly), ZONE 4–9
Lavandula angustifolia (English lavender), ZONE 5–9
Perovskia (Russian sage), ZONE 4–9
Phlomis (Jerusalem sage), ZONE 7–10
Santolina chamaecyparissus (Lavender cotton), ZONE 6–9
Sedum spp. (stonecrop), ZONE 4–9
Stipa tenuissima (Mexican feather grass), ZONE 7–10

About the Author & Photographer

Folko Kullmann
Fascinated by plants since childhood, Folko studied horticulture in the Bavarian town of Freising-Weihenstephan and went on to earn a PhD at the Technical University of Munich. His career has taken him from Europe's largest tree nursery to the Royal Botanic Gardens, Kew, and through a formative traineeship with a Stuttgart reference-book publisher. Since 2004 he has cultivated his passion not only in his own garden and on his balcony but also on the page as a garden journalist, editor, author, translator and creator of gardening books. In 2008 he and his partner established an editorial studio devoted to horticultural books and magazines. He served as president of the German Perennial Society from 2016 until 2024, is editor of the quarterly journal *der Staudengarten* (the perennial garden) and, in 2025, launched his own publishing company, PLANTVS.

Marianne Majerus
One of the world's finest garden photographers with over 35 years of experience, Marianne has photographed many of the world's best gardens, including HRH The Prince of Wales's garden at Highgrove. Winner of many prestigious photography awards, she is a regular contributor to national and international publications, including *House and Garden*, *Gardens Illustrated*, *Country Life*, *Homes and Gardens*, *Country Homes and Interiors*, *The Garden*, *The English Garden*, the *Sunday Times*, the *Guardian* and the *Daily Telegraph*. Marianne has also illustrated over 200 books.

Garden design credits

The gardens in this book were created by the following designers:

Adam Shepherd, The Landscape Architect; pages 169 and 170
Adam Woolcott and Jonathan Smith; pages 134 and 137
Amir Schlezinger, MyLandscapes; pages 65, 66, 67, 164 and 167
Arterra Landscape Architects; pages 149 and 150
Barbara Schwartz; pages 68 and 71
Bunny Guinness Landscape Design; pages 10 (top), 27 and 28
Catherine MacDonald; pages 31 and 32
Charlotte Rowe Garden Design; pages 4, 42, 45, 144 and 147
Claire Mee Designs; pages 186, 189, 194 and 197
Clinton Wootten and Emma Voit; pages 161 and 162
Studio Gazerwitz Landscape Architecture; pages 176 and 179
Dan Cooper Garden; pages 6, 102, 105, 130 and 133
Edwina Roberts; pages 181 and 182
Emma Griffin Garden Design; pages 81, 82, 199 and 200
Gordon McArthur and Paul Thompson; pages 46 and 49
Ian Hammond; pages 107 and 108
James Aldridge Landscape and Garden Design; Pages 39 and 40
James Smith Landscape and Garden Design; pages 202 and 205
Jane Brockbank Gardens; pages, 55, 56, 127 and 128. Pages 11, 94 and 97 **(with John Smart Architects)**
Juan Carlos Cure; front cover
Lynne Marcus Garden Design; pages 76 and 79
Luis Buitrago, John Nicolson; pages 110 and 113
Maurizio Vegini, Studio GPT; pages 173 and 174. Furniture by Gaetano Pesce, 'La Tempesta' (1981) wall art by Francesco Somaini
Peter Berg Garden Design; pages 114 and 117
Rodney Archer; pages 99 and 100
Sara Jane Rothwell, London Garden Designer; pages 73, 75 and 213
Shades of Green Landscape Architecture; pages 60 and 63
Spencer Viner; pages 152, 154 and 155
Stephen Smith; pages 91 and 92
Steve Buckley; pages 139, 140 and 141 (sculptures by Steve Buckley)
Stuart Craine Design; pages 22, 25, 119, 120, 157, 159, 206 and 209
Sue Townsend Garden Design; pages 14, 17 (screen by Steel Sculptures), 122, 125 and back cover
Tony Woods, Garden Club London; pages 9, 10 (bottom), 34, 37, 51, 52, 84, 87, 191 and 192. Pages 18 and 21 **(with Smith and Butler)**

Acknowledgements

A book, like a garden, flourishes only through many devoted hands, and I am indebted to each one. My heartfelt thanks go first to Roly Allen, whose foresight reunited us after almost two decades and planted the initial seed of this collaboration. I am equally grateful to Zara Larcombe and Virginia Brehaut from Skittledog for their patience and creativity. Gaynor Sermon's meticulous edits, finely tuned questions and quiet diligence lifted every line, while Sara Harper applied a keen eye in proofreading, ensuring each page is as polished as a well-kept border. With deft skill, Sarah Pyke combined text and image into a harmonious layout, bringing the entire project into bloom. Marianne Majerus contributed her consistently breathtaking photographs, capturing the soul of every small garden featured here. Above all, my partner Kristijan has unfailingly had my back, and my grandmothers and parents nurtured my early fascination with plants, supporting my path in gardening. To all of you, thank you for helping this book take root and thrive.

First published in the United Kingdom in 2026
by Skittledog, an imprint of Thames & Hudson Ltd,
6–24 Britannia Street, London WC1X 9JD

Senior Editor: Virginia Brehaut
Designer: Sarah Pyke
Production: Felicity Awdry

Photographer portrait on page 214 by Cantra Clark

EU Authorized Representative: Interart S.A.R.L.
19 rue Charles Auray, 93500 Pantin, Paris, France
productsafety@thameshudson.co.uk
www.interart.fr

A CIP catalogue record for this book is available from the British Library

ISBN 978-1-83776-059-6
01

Printed and bound in China by C&C Offset Printing Co., Ltd